Richard Harwood and Ian Lodge

Cambridge IGCSE®

Physical Science

Chemistry Workbook

T0159710

CAMBRIDGE
UNIVERSITY PRESS

CAMBRIDGE
UNIVERSITY PRESS

University Printing House, Cambridge CB2 8BS, United Kingdom

One Liberty Plaza, 20th Floor, New York, NY 10006, USA

477 Williamstown Road, Port Melbourne, VIC 3207, Australia

4843/24, 2nd Floor, Ansari Road, Daryaganj, Delhi – 110002, India

79 Anson Road, #06–04/06, Singapore 079906

Cambridge University Press is part of the University of Cambridge.

It furthers the University's mission by disseminating knowledge in the pursuit of education, learning and research at the highest international levels of excellence.

www.cambridge.org
Information on this title: www.cambridge.org/9781316633519

© Cambridge University Press 2017

This publication is in copyright. Subject to statutory exception and to the provisions of relevant collective licensing agreements, no reproduction of any part may take place without the written permission of Cambridge University Press.

First published 2017
20 19 18 17 16 15 14 13 12 11 10 9 8 7 6 5 4 3 2 1

Printed in Malaysia by Vivar Printing

A catalogue record for this publication is available from the British Library

ISBN 978-1-316-63351-9 Paperback

Cambridge University Press has no responsibility for the persistence or accuracy of URLs for external or third-party internet websites referred to in this publication, and does not guarantee that any content on such websites is, or will remain, accurate or appropriate. Information regarding prices, travel timetables, and other factual information given in this work is correct at the time of first printing but Cambridge University Press does not guarantee the accuracy of such information thereafter.

....

NOTICE TO TEACHERS IN THE UK
It is illegal to reproduce any part of this work in material form (including photocopying and electronic storage) except under the following circumstances:
(i)   where you are abiding by a licence granted to your school or institution by the Copyright Licensing Agency;
(ii) where no such licence exists, or where you wish to exceed the terms of a licence, and you have gained the written permission of Cambridge University Press;
(iii) where you are allowed to reproduce without permission under the provisions of Chapter 3 of the Copyright, Designs and Patents Act 1988, which covers, for example, the reproduction of short passages within certain types of educational anthology and reproduction for the purposes of setting examination questions.

® IGCSE is the registered trademark of Cambridge International Examinations.

Example answers and all questions were written by the authors.

This workbook contains exercises designed to help you develop the skills needed for success in Cambridge IGCSE® Physical Science.

The examination tests three different Assessment Objectives, or AOs for short. These are:

AO1 Knowledge with understanding

AO2 Handling information and problem solving

AO3 Experimental skills and investigations.

In the examination, about 50% of the marks are for AO1, 30% for AO2 and 20% for AO3. Just learning your work and remembering it is therefore not enough to make sure that you get the best possible grade in the exam. Half of all the marks are for AO2 and AO3. You need to be able to use what you've learnt in unfamiliar contexts (AO2) and to demonstrate your experimental skills (AO3).

This workbook contains exercises to help you to develop AO2 and AO3 further. There are some questions that just involve remembering things you have been taught (AO1), but most of the questions require you to use what you've learnt to work out, for example, what a set of data means, or to suggest how an experiment might be improved.

These exercises are not intended to be exactly like the questions you will get on your exam papers. This is because they are meant to help you to develop your skills, rather than testing you on them.

There's an introduction at the start of each exercise that tells you the purpose of it – which skills you will be working with as you answer the questions.

For some parts of the exercises, there are self-assessment checklists. You can try marking your own work using these. This will help you to remember the important points to think about. Your teacher should also mark the work and will discuss with you whether your own assessments are right.

The exercises cover both Core and Supplement material of the syllabus. The Supplement material can be identified by the Supplement bar in the margin (as shown). This indicates that the exercise is intended for students who are studying the Supplement content of the syllabus as well as the Core.

The Periodic Table of Elements

Group

I	II		III	IV	V	VI	VII	VIII
								2 **He** helium 4
3 **Li** lithium 7	4 **Be** beryllium 9		5 **B** boron 11	6 **C** carbon 12	7 **N** nitrogen 14	8 **O** oxygen 16	9 **F** fluorine 19	10 **Ne** neon 20
11 **Na** sodium 23	12 **Mg** magnesium 24		13 **Al** aluminium 27	14 **Si** silicon 28	15 **P** phosphorus 31	16 **S** sulfur 32	17 **Cl** chlorine 35.5	18 **Ar** argon 40

19 **K** potassium 39	20 **Ca** calcium 40	21 **Sc** scandium 45	22 **Ti** titanium 48	23 **V** vanadium 51	24 **Cr** chromium 52	25 **Mn** manganese 55	26 **Fe** iron 56	27 **Co** cobalt 59	28 **Ni** nickel 59	29 **Cu** copper 64	30 **Zn** zinc 65
37 **Rb** rubidium 85	38 **Sr** strontium 88	39 **Y** yttrium 89	40 **Zr** zirconium 91	41 **Nb** niobium 93	42 **Mo** molybdenum 96	43 **Tc** technetium -	44 **Ru** ruthenium 101	45 **Rh** rhodium 103	46 **Pd** palladium 106	47 **Ag** silver 108	48 **Cd** cadmium 112
55 **Cs** caesium 133	56 **Ba** barium 137	57–71 lanthanoids	72 **Hf** hafnium 179	73 **Ta** tantalum 181	74 **W** tungsten 184	75 **Re** rhenium 186	76 **Os** osmium 190	77 **Ir** iridium 192	78 **Pt** platinum 195	79 **Au** gold 197	80 **Hg** mercury 201
87 **Fr** francium -	88 **Ra** radium -	89–103 actinoids	104 **Rf** rutherfordium -	105 **Db** dubnium -	106 **Sg** seaborgium -	107 **Bh** bohrium -	108 **Hs** hassium -	109 **Mt** meitnerium -	110 **Ds** darmstadtium -	111 **Rg** roentgenium -	112 **Cn** copernicium -

Continued Group columns III–VIII for periods 4–7:

III	IV	V	VI	VII	VIII
31 **Ga** gallium 70	32 **Ge** germanium 73	33 **As** arsenic 75	34 **Se** aelenium 79	35 **Br** bromine 80	36 **Kr** krypton 84
49 **In** indium 115	50 **Sn** tin 119	51 **Sb** antimony 122	52 **Te** tellurium 128	53 **I** iodine 127	54 **Xe** xenon 131
81 **Tl** thallium 204	82 **Pb** lead 207	83 **Bi** bismuth 209	84 **Po** polonium -	85 **At** astatine -	86 **Rn** radon -
	114 **Fl** flerovium -		116 **Lv** livermorium -		

Key

atomic number
atomic symbol
name
relative atomic mass

1 **H** hydrogen 1

lanthanoids

| 57
LA
lanthanium
139 | 58
Ce
cerium
140 | 59
Pr
praseodymium
141 | 60
Nd
neodymium
144 | 61
Pm
promethium
- | 62
Sm
samarium
150 | 63
Eu
europium
152 | 64
Gd
gadolinium
157 | 65
Tb
terbium
159 | 66
Dy
dysprosium
163 | 67
Ho
holmium
165 | 68
Er
erbium
167 | 69
Tm
thulium
169 | 70
Yb
ytterbium
173 | 71
Lu
lutetium
175 |

actinoids

| 89
AC
actinium
- | 90
Th
thorium
232 | 91
Pa
protactinium
231 | 92
U
uranium
238 | 93
Np
neptunium
- | 94
Pu
plutonium
- | 95
Am
americium
- | 96
Cm
curium
- | 97
Bk
berkelium
- | 98
Cf
californium
- | 99
Es
einsteinium
- | 100
Fm
fermium
- | 101
Md
mendelevium
- | 102
No
nobelium
- | 103
Lr
lawrencium
- |

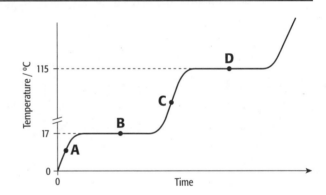

DEFINITIONS TO LEARN

physical state: the three states of matter are solid, liquid and gas

condensation: the change of state from gas to liquid

melting: the change of state from solid to liquid

freezing: the change of state from liquid to solid at the melting point

boiling: the change of state from liquid to gas at the boiling point of the liquid

evaporation: the change of state from liquid to gas below the boiling point

sublimation: the change of state directly from solid to gas (or the reverse)

crystallisation: the formation of crystals when a saturated solution is left to cool

Exercise C1.1 Changing physical state

> This exercise will develop your understanding of the kinetic model and the energy changes involved in changes of physical state.

The graph shows the heating curve for a pure substance. The temperature rises with time as the substance is heated.

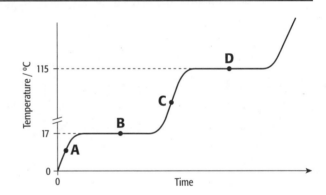

a What physical state(s) is the substance in at points A, B, C and D?

A ....   C ....

B ....   D ....

b What is the melting point of the substance? ....

c What is its boiling point? ....

d What happens to the temperature while the substance is changing state?

....

e The substance is not water. How do we know this from the graph?

....

f Complete the passage using the words given below.

different	**diffusion**	**gas**	**spread**	**particles**
diffuse	**random**	**lattice**	**vibrate**	**temperature**

The kinetic **model** states that the .... in a liquid and a ....
are in constant motion. In a gas, the particles are far apart from each other and their motion is said to be
.... The particles in a solid are held in fixed positions in a regular
.... In a solid, the particles can only .... about their fixed
positions.

Liquids and gases are fluid states. When particles move in a fluid, they can collide with each other. When
they collide, they bounce off each other in .... directions. If two gases or liquids are
mixed, the different types of particle .... out and get mixed up. This process is called
....

At the same .... particles that have a lower mass move faster than those with higher
mass. This means that the lighter particles will spread and mix more quickly; the lighter particles are said to
...................................faster than the heavier particles.

g Use the data given for the substances listed below to answer the questions that follow on their physical state at
a room temperature of 25 °C and atmospheric pressure.

Substance	Melting point/°C	Boiling point/°C
sodium	98	883
radon	−71	−62
ethanol	−117	78
cobalt	1492	2900
nitrogen	−210	−196
propane	−188	−42
ethanoic acid	16	118

i   Which substance is a liquid over the smallest range of temperature? ....

ii   Which **two** substances are gaseous at –50 °C?

         .... and ....

iii   Which substance has the lowest freezing point? ....

iv   Which substance is liquid at 2500 °C? ....

v   A sample of ethanoic acid was found to boil at 121 °C at atmospheric pressure. Use the information in the table to comment on this result.

         ....

         ....

Exercise C1.2   Plotting a cooling curve

> **This exercise presents data obtained practically for plotting a cooling curve. It will help develop your skills in handling the data and interpreting what changes the different regions of the curve represent. Examples of sublimation are also discussed.**

A student, carried out the following data-logging experiment using the apparatus shown below, as part of a project on changes of state. An organic crystalline solid was melted by placing it in a tube in a boiling water bath. A temperature sensor was placed in the sample tube.

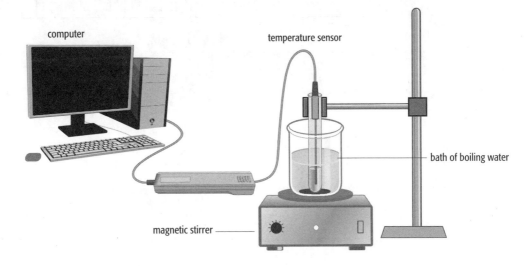

The temperature change was followed as the liquid was allowed to cool down. The data shown in the table below are taken from the computer record of the temperature change as the liquid cooled down to room temperature.

Time / min	0	0.5	1.0	1.5	2.0	2.2	2.4	2.6	2.8	3.0	3.5	4.0	4.5	5.0
Temperature / °C	96.1	89.2	85.2	82.0	80.9	80.7	80.6	80.6	80.5	80.3	78.4	74.2	64.6	47.0

3

a   On the grid below, plot a graph of the temperature change taking place in this experiment.

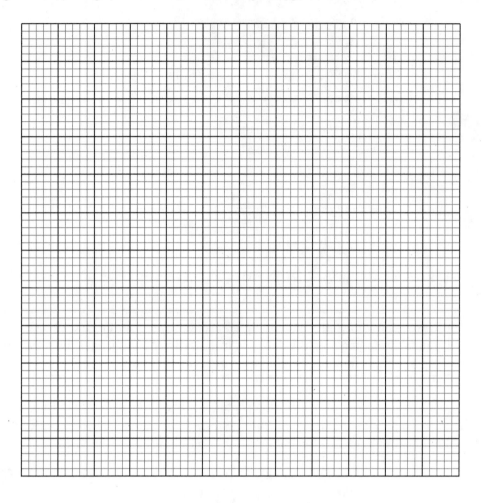

b   What change is taking place over the second minute of the experiment?

....

c   Why does the temperature remain almost constant over this period of time? Give your explanation in terms of what is happening to the organisation of the molecules of the substance.

....

....

....

....

d What change would need to be made to carry out the experiment using a compound with a melting point greater than 100 °C?

....

e A similar experiment was carried out to demonstrate the cooling curve for paraffin wax.

    i In the space below, sketch the shape of the graph you would expect to produce.

    ii Explain why the curve is the shape you have drawn.

    ....

    ....

5

f Sublimation occurs when a substance passes between the solid and gaseous states without going through the liquid phase. Both carbon dioxide and water can sublime under certain conditions of temperature and pressure.

'Dry ice' is the solid form of carbon dioxide used in commercial refrigeration. At atmospheric pressure it has a 'sublimation point' of −78.5 °C.

    i What difference can you see between solid carbon dioxide and water ice at atmospheric pressure?

    ....

    ....

    ii If you gently shake a carbon dioxide fire extinguisher, you will feel the presence of liquid within the extinguisher. What conditions within the extinguisher mean that the CO_2 is liquid in this case?

    ....

    ....

iii   Complete the following paragraph about a particular type of frost using the words listed below.

surrounding   liquid   colder   humid

white   crystals   ice

Hoar frost is a powdery .... frost caused when solid .... forms from .... air. The solid surface on which it is formed must be .... than the .... air. Water vapour is deposited on a surface as fine ice .... without going through the .... phase.

DEFINITIONS TO LEARN

filtration: the separation of a solid from a liquid using filter paper

distillation: the separation of a liquid from a mixture using differences in boiling point

fractional distillation: the separation of a mixture of liquids using differences in boiling point

diffusion: the random movement of particles in a fluid (liquid or gas) leading to the complete mixing of the particles

chromatography: the separation of a mixture of soluble (coloured) substances using paper and a solvent

Exercise C2.1 Diffusion, solubility and separation

The processes of diffusion and dissolving in a solvent are linked. This exercise explores the basis of these processes in terms of the kinetic (particle) theory. The separation of a solvent mixture by fractional distillation is also discussed.

A student placed some crystals of potassium manganate(VII) at the bottom of a beaker of distilled water. She then left the contents of the beaker to stand for one hour.

a The diagram below shows what she saw during the experiment.

After one hour, all the solid crystals had disappeared and the solution was purple throughout.

distilled water

purple crystals

   at start   after 15 minutes   after one hour

 i Use the ideas of the kinetic theory to explain her observations.

....

....

....

....

....

 ii If warm water at 50 °C had been used, would the observations have taken place in a longer or shorter time? Explain your answer.

....

....

....

b The process of dissolving can be used to separate and purify chemical compounds. Organic solvents such as propanone can be used to extract pigments from plants. Some grass is crushed and mixed with the propanone. The colour pigments are extracted to give a dark green solution.

  i Given a pure sample of chlorophyll, describe how could you show that the green solution from the grass contained chlorophyll and other coloured pigments?

  ....

  ....

  ....

  ....

  ii Draw a labelled diagram that describes the method of separating coloured pigments that you have discussed in part **i**.

Use the checklist below to give yourself a mark for your drawing. For each point, award yourself:

- 2 marks if you did it really well
- 1 mark if you made a good attempt at it, and partly succeeded
- 0 marks if you did not try to do it, or did not succeed.

Self-assessment checklist for drawings

Check point	Marks awarded	
	You	Your teacher
You have made a large drawing, using the space provided.		
There are no obvious errors – liquids missing, flasks open when they should be closed, etc.		
You have drawn single lines with a sharp pencil, not many tries at the same line (and erased mistakes).		
You have used a ruler for the lines that are straight.		
Your diagram is in the right proportions.		
You have drawn label lines with a ruler, touching the item being labelled.		
You have written the labels horizontally and neatly, well away from the diagram itself.		
Total (out of 14)		

12–14   Excellent.

10–11   Good.

7–9   A good start, but you need to improve quite a bit.

5–6   Poor. Try this same drawing again, using a new sheet of paper.

1–4   Very poor. Read through all the criteria again, and then try the same drawing.

c Propanone is a very useful solvent that mixes well with water even though it is an organic compound. A propanone:water (65%:35%) mixture used for cleaning laboratory apparatus can be separated using fractional distillation.

A total volume of 80 cm³ of the mixture was distilled.

Sketch below a graph of the temperature readings against the volume of distillate collected for the distillation carried out. The thermometer is placed at the connection between the fractionating column and the condenser. The boiling point of propanone is 56 °C.

Exercise C2.2 Chromatography at the races

> **This exercise will help you understand aspects of chromatography by considering an unfamiliar application of the technique.**

Chromatography is used by the 'Horse Racing Forensic Laboratory' to test for the presence of illegal drugs in racehorses.

A concentrated sample of urine is spotted on to chromatography paper on the start line. Alongside this, known drugs are spotted. The chromatogram is run using methanol as the solvent. When finished, the paper is read by placing it under ultraviolet light. A chromatogram of urine from four racehorses is shown below.

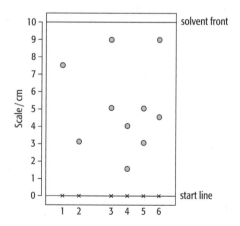

Spot	Description
1	caffeine
2	paracetamol
3	urine sample horse A
4	urine sample horse B
5	urine sample horse C
6	urine sample horse D

a State **two** factors which determine the distance a substance travels up the paper.

....

....

b The results show that the sample from one horse contains an illegal substance. State which horse and the drug that is present.

....

c Give a reason for the use of this drug.

....

d The results for known drugs are given as 'R_f values'.

$$R_f = \frac{\text{distance travelled by the substance}}{\text{distance travelled by the solvent}}$$

Calculate the R_f value for caffeine.

C3:
Atoms, elements and compounds

 DEFINITIONS TO LEARN

atom: the smallest part of an element that can take part in a chemical change

proton number (atomic number): the number of protons in the nucleus of an atom of an element

nucleon number (mass number): the number of protons and neutrons in the nucleus of an atom

electron arrangement: the organisation of electrons in their different energy levels (shells)

isotopes: atoms of the same element which have the same proton number but a different nucleon number

element: a substance containing only one type of atom

compound: a substance made of two, or more, elements chemically combined together

Periodic Table: the table in which the elements are organised in order of increasing proton number and electron arrangement

group: a vertical column of elements in the Periodic Table; elements in the same group have similar properties

period: a horizontal row of elements in the Periodic Table

valency: the number of chemical bonds an atom can make

Exercise C3.1 Atomic structure

This exercise helps familiarise you with aspects of atomic structure including the organisation of electrons into energy levels (or shells), and the uses of radioactivity.

a Choose from the words below to fill in the gaps in the passage. Words may be used once, more than once or not at all.

proton	electrons	nucleon	isotopes	protons

neutrons	nucleus	energy levels

Atoms are made up of three different particles: .... which are positively charged; .... which have no charge; and .... which are negatively charged.

The negatively charged particles are arranged in different .... (shells) around the .... of the atom. The particles with a negligible mass are the .... All atoms of the same element contain the same number of .... and .... Atoms of the same element with different numbers of .... are known as ....

b This part of the exercise is concerned with electron arrangements and the structure of the Periodic Table. Complete these sentences by filling in the blanks with words or numbers.

The electrons in an atom are arranged in a series of .... around the nucleus. These shells are

also called .... levels. In an atom, the shell .... to the nucleus fills first,

then the next shell, and so on. There is room for:

* up to .... electrons in the first shell
* up to .... electrons in the second shell
* up to .... electrons in the third shell.

(There are 18 electrons in total when the three shells are completely full.)

The elements in the Periodic Table are organised in the same way as the electrons fill the shells. Shells fill from

.... to .... across the .... of the Periodic Table.

* The first shell fills up first from .... to helium.
* The second shell fills next from lithium to ....
* Eight .... go into the third shell from sodium to argon.
* Then the fourth shell starts to fill from potassium.

Exercise C3.2 The first four periods

> **This exercise is aimed at developing your knowledge of the basic features of the Periodic Table and the properties of an element that relate to its position in the table.**

The diagram below shows the upper part of the Periodic Table with certain elements selected.

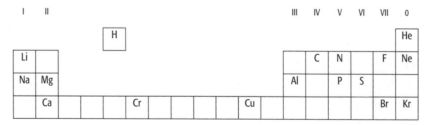

Using the elements shown above, write down the symbols for the elements which answer the following questions.

a   Which **two** elements are stored under oil because they are very reactive?

   ....

b   Which **two** elements are transition metals?

   ....

c   Which element has just two electrons in the full outer shell of its atom?

   ....

d   Which element is a red-brown liquid at room temperature and pressure?

   ....

e   Which element has four electrons in the outer energy level of its atom?

   ....

f   Which element is a yellow solid at room temperature?

   ....

g   Which elements are noble gases?

   ....

h   Which element has compounds that produce blue solutions when they dissolve?

   ....

i   Which element has the electron arrangement 2.8.8.2?

   ....

j   Which element burns with a brilliant white flame when ignited?

   ....

Exercise C3.3 The chemical bonding in simple molecules

> This exercise will familiarise you with the structures of some simple covalent compounds and the methods we have for representing the structure and shape of their molecules.

a   Many covalent compounds exist as simple molecules where the atoms are joined together with single or double bonds. A covalent bond, made up of a shared pair of electrons, is often represented by a short straight line. Complete the table by filling in the blank spaces.

Name of compound	Formula	Drawing of structure	Molecular model
hydrogen chloride	....	H — C*l*	
water	H_2O	O ∕ ∖ H H	
ammonia			
....	CH_4		
ethene	....	H H ∖ ∕ C＝C ∕ ∖ H H	
....	....	O＝C＝O	

b   Graphite is one of the crystalline forms of carbon. Two of the distinctive properties of graphite are:

- it conducts electricity even though it is a non-metal, and
- it can act as a lubricant even though it has a giant covalent structure.

Give a brief explanation of these properties in the light of the structure of graphite.

i   Graphite as an electrical conductor

....

....

....

ii   Graphite as a lubricant

....

....

....

15

Exercise C3.4 The nature of ionic lattices

This exercise will help you relate the structures of ionic compounds to some of their key properties.

The diagram shows a model of the structure of sodium chloride and similar ionic crystals. The ions are arranged in a regular lattice structure – a giant ionic lattice.

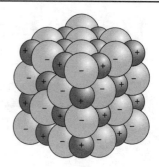

The boxes below contain properties of ionic compounds and their explanations. Draw lines to link each pair.

Property

The solution of an ionic compound in water is a good conductor of electricity – such ionic substances are electrolytes.

Ionic crystals have a regular shape. All the crystals of each solid ionic compound are the same shape. Whatever the size of the crystal, the angles between the faces of the crystal are always the same.

Ionic compounds have relatively high melting points.

When an ionic compound is heated above its melting point, the molten compound is a good conductor of electricity.

Explanation

The ions in the giant ionic structure are always arranged in the same regular way – see the diagram.

The giant ionic structure is held together by the strong attraction between the positive and negative ions. It takes a lot of energy to break down the regular arrangement of ions.

In a molten ionic compound, the positive and negative ions can move around – they can move to the electrodes when a voltage is applied.

In a solution of an ionic compound, the positive metal ions and the negative non-metal ions can move around – they can move to the electrodes when a voltage is applied.

indicator: a substance that changes colour depending on whether it is in an acid or alkali

salt: an ionic substance produced from an acid by neutralisation with a base

neutralisation reaction: a reaction between an acid and a base to produce a salt and water only

relative atomic mass: the average mass of naturally occurring atoms of an element on a scale where the carbon-12 atom has a mass of exactly 12 units

relative formula mass: the sum of all the relative atomic masses of all the atoms or ions in a compound

chemical formula: the formula of an ionic compound shows the ratio of the atoms in a compound in whole numbers; for a simple covalent compound the formula shows the numbers of each atom present in the molecule.

mole: the relative formula mass of a substance in grams

molar gas volume: the volume occupied by one mole of any gas ($24\,dm^3$ at room temperature and pressure)

Exercise C4.1 Formulae of ionic compounds

The writing of chemical formulae is central to chemistry. This exercise will help you understand how to work out the formulae of ionic compounds and what such formulae mean.

The table below shows the valencies and formulae of some common ions.

		Valency		
		1	**2**	**3**
Positive ions (cations)	**metals**	sodium (Na^+) potassium (K^+) silver (Ag^+)	magnesium (Mg^{2+}) copper (Cu^{2+}) zinc (Zn^{2+}) iron (Fe^{2+})	aluminium (Al^{3+}) iron (Fe^{3+}) chromium (Cr^{3+})
	compound ions	ammonium (NH_4^+)		
Negative ions (anions)	**non-metals**	chloride (Cl^-) bromide (Br^-) iodide (I^-)	oxide (O^{2-}) sulfide (S^{2-})	nitride (N^{3-})
	compound ions	nitrate (NO_3^-) hydroxide (OH^-)	carbonate (CO_3^{2-}) sulfate (SO_4^{2-})	phosphate (PO_4^{3-})

a Use the information in the table to work out the formulae of the following ionic compounds.

   i   Copper oxide   ....

   ii   Sodium carbonate   ....

   iii   Zinc sulfate   ....

   iv   Silver nitrate   ....

   v   Magnesium bromide   ....

   vi   Ammonium sulfate   ....

   vii   Magnesium nitride   ....

   viii Potassium phosphate   ....

   ix   Iron(III) hydroxide   ....

   x   Chromium(III) chloride   ....

b Use the information in the table and your answers in **a** above to give the ratio of the different atoms in the following compounds.

   i   Copper oxide   Cu : O   ....

   ii   Magnesium bromide   Mg : Br   ....

   iii   Magnesium nitride   Mg : N   ....

   iv   Iron(III) hydroxide   Fe : O : H   ....

   v   Ammonium sulfate   N : H : S : O ....

c The diagram below shows a representation of the structure of an ionic oxide.

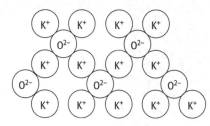

   i   What is the ratio of K^+ ions to O^{2-} ions? ....

   ii   What is the formula of this compound? ....

18

d The following diagram shows the structure of common salt.

   i Extend the structure to the right, by adding **four** more ions.

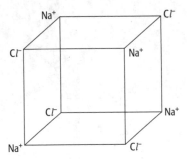

   ii Complete the diagrams below for the ions in the structure to show their electron arrangement. Draw in any missing electron shells, showing clearly the origin of the electrons involved.

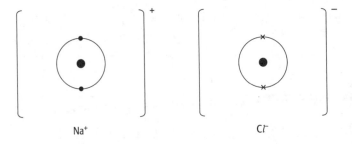

   iii Draw an ionic diagram similar to the one above for the structure of magnesium chloride.

Exercise C4.2 Making magnesium oxide – a quantitative investigation

> **This exercise will develop your skills in processing and interpreting results from practical work.**

Magnesium oxide is made when magnesium is burnt in air. How does the mass of magnesium oxide made depend on the mass of magnesium burnt? The practical method is described below.

Method

- Weigh an empty crucible and lid.
- Roll some magnesium ribbon around a pencil, then remove the coiled ribbon and place it in the crucible and re-weigh (not forgetting the lid).
- Place the crucible in a pipeclay triangle sitting safely on a tripod. (The lid should be on the crucible.)
- Heat the crucible and contents strongly, occasionally lifting the lid to allow more air in.
- When the reaction has eased, take off the lid.
- Heat strongly for another three minutes.
- Let the crucible cool down and then weigh it.
- Repeat the heating until the mass is constant.

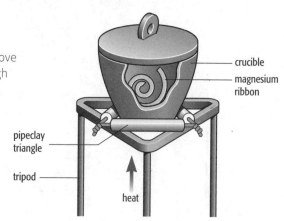

Results

The table shows a set of class results calculated from the weights each student group obtained using this method.

Mass of magnesium / g	0.06	0.05	0.04	0.18	0.16	0.10	0.11	0.14	0.15	0.14	0.08	0.10	0.13
Mass of magnesium oxide / g	0.10	0.08	0.06	0.28	0.25	0.15	0.15	0.21	0.24	0.23	0.13	0.17	0.21

Use these results to plot a graph on the grid below relating mass of magnesium oxide made to mass of magnesium used. Remember there is one point on this graph that you can be certain of – what point is that? Include it on your graph.

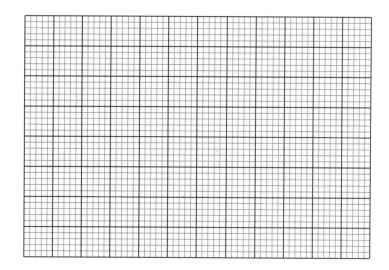

Use the checklist below to give yourself a mark for your graph. For each point, award yourself:

- 2 marks if you did it really well
- 1 mark if you made a good attempt at it, and partly succeeded
- 0 marks if you did not try to do it, or did not succeed.

Self-assessment checklist for graphs:

Check point	Marks awarded	
	You	Your teacher
You have drawn the axes with a ruler, using most of the width and height of the grid.		
You have used a good scale for the x-axis and the y-axis, going up in 0.01 s, 0.05 s or 0.10 s.		
You have labelled the axes correctly, giving the correct units for the scales on both axes.		
You have plotted each point precisely and correctly.		
You have used a small, neat cross for each point.		
You have drawn a single, clear best-fit line through the points – using a ruler for a straight line.		
You have ignored any anomalous results when drawing the line.		
Total (out of 14)		

12–14	Excellent.
10–11	Good.
7–9	A good start, but you need to improve quite a bit.
5–6	Poor. Try this same graph again, using a new sheet of graph paper.
1–4	Very poor. Read through all the criteria again, and then try the same graph again.

a How does the mass of magnesium oxide relate to the starting mass of magnesium?

....

b Work out from the graph the mass of magnesium oxide that you would get from 0.12 g of magnesium (show the

lines you use for this on your graph)....................................... g

c What mass of oxygen combines with 0.12 g of magnesium?.................................... g

d What mass of oxygen combines with 24 g of magnesium?.................................... g

e What is the formula of magnesium oxide, worked out on the basis of these results?
(Relative atomic masses: Mg = 24, O = 16.)

....

....

Exercise C4.3 The analysis of titration results

> This exercise will develop your understanding of some of the practical skills involved in acid–base titrations and the processing and evaluation of experimental results.

A student investigated an aqueous solution of sodium hydroxide and its reaction with hydrochloric acid. He carried out two experiments.

Experiment 1

Using a measuring cylinder, 10 cm³ of the sodium hydroxide solution was placed in a conical flask. Methyl orange indicator was added to the flask. A burette was filled to the 0.0 cm³ mark with hydrochloric acid (solution **P**).

The student added solution **P** slowly to the alkali in the flask until the colour just changed. Use the burette diagram to record the volume in the results table and then complete the column for experiment **1**.

Experiment 1 final reading

Experiment 2

Experiment **1** was repeated using a different solution of hydrochloric acid (solution **Q**).

Use the burette diagrams to record the volumes in the results table and complete the column.

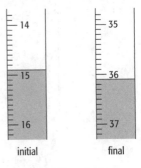

initial   final

Experiment 2 readings

Table of results

Burette readings / cm³	Experiment 1	Experiment 2
final reading	....	....
initial reading	0.0	....
difference	....	....

a What type of chemical reaction occurs when hydrochloric acid reacts with sodium hydroxide?

....

b Write a word equation for the reaction.

....

c What was the colour change of the indicator observed?

....

d Which of the experiments used the greater volume of hydrochloric acid?

....

e Compare the volumes of acid used in experiments **1** and **2** and suggest an explanation for the difference between the volumes.

....

....

23

f Predict the volume of hydrochloric acid **P** that would be needed to react completely if experiment **1** was repeated with 25 cm³ of sodium hydroxide solution.

Volume of solution needed: ....
Explanation

....

g Suggest **one** change the student could make to the **apparatus** used in order to obtain more accurate results.

....

Exercise C4.4 Calculating formula masses

This exercise will develop your understanding and recall of the ideas about atomic and formula mass.

a Complete the following diagram by filling in the blanks.

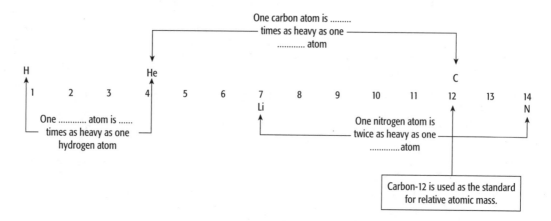

b Complete the following table of formula masses for a range of different types of substance.

(Relative atomic masses: O = 16, H = 1, C = 12, N = 14, Ca = 40, Mg = 24)

Molecule	Chemical formula	Number of atoms or ions involved	Relative formula mass
oxygen	O_2	2 O	$2 \times 16 = 32$
carbon dioxide	....	1 C and 2 O	$1 \times 12 + 2 \times 16 =$....................
....	H_2O	2 H and 1....................	....................=....................
ammonia	....	1 N and 3 H	....................=....................
calcium carbonate	....	1 Ca^{2+} and 1 CO_3^{2-}	..........+..........+$3 \times 16 = 100$
....	MgO	1 Mg^{2+} and 1 O^{2-}	$1 \times 24 + 1 \times 16 =$..........
ammonium nitrate	NH_4NO_3	1 NH_4^+ and	$2 \times 14 +$....................+ ....$= 80$
propanol	C_3H_7OH	3 C, ...and	$3 \times 12 + 8 \times 1 +$..........=..........

Exercise C4.5 A sense of proportion in chemistry

> This exercise will familiarise you with some of the basic calculations involved in chemistry.

a Zinc metal is extracted from its oxide. In the industrial extraction process, 5 tonnes of zinc oxide are needed to produce 4 tonnes of zinc. Calculate the mass of zinc, in tonnes, that is produced from 20 tonnes of zinc oxide.

b Nitrogen and hydrogen react together to form ammonia.

$$N_2 + 3H_2 \rightarrow 2NH_3$$

When the reaction is complete, 14 tonnes of nitrogen are converted into 17 tonnes of ammonia.

How much nitrogen will be needed to produce 34 tonnes of ammonia?

c The sugar lactose, $C_{12}H_{22}O_{11}$, is sometimes used in place of charcoal in fireworks.

State the total number of atoms present in a molecule of lactose. ....

d A molecule of compound **Y** contains the following atoms bonded covalently together:

- 2 atoms of carbon (C)

- 2 atoms of oxygen (O)

- 4 atoms of hydrogen (H).

What is the formula of a molecule of **Y**? ....

Exercise C4.6 Finding the mass of 5 cm of magnesium ribbon

This exercise will develop your skills in handling experimental data in novel situations.

From the chemical equation for the reaction and using the relative formula masses together with the molar volume of a gas it is possible to predict the amounts of magnesium sulfate and hydrogen that are produced when 24 g of magnesium are reacted with excess sulfuric acid.

This relationship between the mass of magnesium used and the volume of gas produced can be used to find the mass of a short piece of magnesium ribbon indirectly.

Apparatus and method

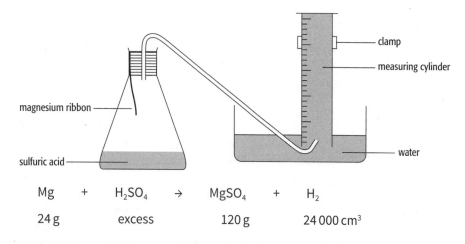

Mg	+	H_2SO_4	$\rightarrow$	$MgSO_4$	+	H_2
24 g		excess		120 g		24 000 cm^3

The experimental instructions were as follows.

- Wear safety goggles for eye protection.
- Set up the apparatus as shown in the diagram with 25 cm^3 of sulfuric acid in the flask.
- Make sure the measuring cylinder is completely full of water.
- Carefully measure 5 cm of magnesium ribbon and grip it below the flask stopper as shown.
- Ease the stopper up to release the ribbon and immediately replace the stopper.
- When no further bubbles rise into the measuring cylinder, record the volume of gas collected.
- Repeat the experiment twice more using 5 cm of magnesium ribbon and fresh sulfuric acid each time.
- Find the average volume of hydrogen produced.

Data handling

A student obtained the results shown in the table when measuring the volume of hydrogen produced.

Experiment number	Volume of hydrogen collected / cm³
1	85
2	79
3	82
average	....

a What mass of magnesium, when placed in excess sulfuric acid has produced the average volume of hydrogen recorded by this student.

....

b You know that 24 g of magnesium will produce 24 000 cm³ of hydrogen. What mass of magnesium would be needed to produce your volume of hydrogen?

....

....

The mass you calculated above is for 5 cm of magnesium ribbon. The weight is too low to weigh easily on a balance but you could weigh a longer length and use that to check your answer.

c What mass of magnesium sulfate would you expect 5 cm of magnesium ribbon to produce?

....

....

d Plan an experiment to check whether your prediction above is correct.

....

....

....

....

....

....

Exercise C4.7   Reacting volumes of gases

There is a direct relationship between the volume of a gas and the number of moles present in the sample. This exercise gives you an example of how to use that relationship for a particular experiment.

Experiments show that volumes of gases react together in a ratio that can be predicted from the chemical equation for the reaction.

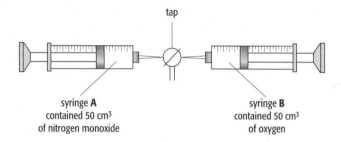

tap

syringe **A**
contained 50 cm³
of nitrogen monoxide

syringe **B**
contained 50 cm³
of oxygen

Under the conditions used here, nitrogen monoxide (NO) reacts with oxygen (O_2) to form one product that is a brown gas. In an experiment, 5.0 cm³ portions of oxygen were pushed from syringe **B** into syringe **A**.

After each addition, the tap was closed, the gases were cooled, and then the total volume of gases remaining was measured. The results are shown in the graph.

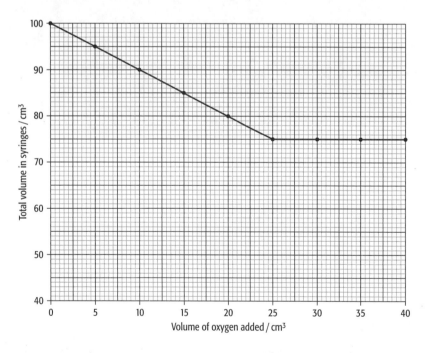

a   What is the total volume of gases when the reaction is complete?

....

b   What volume of oxygen reacts with 50 cm³ of nitrogen monoxide?

....

c   What is the volume of the brown gas formed?

....

d   Complete the following to work out the formula of the brown gas:

$$\text{............ NO} \quad + \quad O_2 \quad \rightarrow \quad \text{............}$$

$$50\ cm^3 \qquad\qquad \text{...... } cm^3 \qquad\qquad \text{...... } cm^3$$

DEFINITIONS TO LEARN

synthesis: the formation of a more complex compound from its elements (or simple substances)

decomposition: the breakdown of a compound into simpler substances

precipitation: the sudden, immediate formation of a solid during a chemical reaction

oxidation: the addition of oxygen to an element or compound

reduction: the removal of oxygen from a compound

redox reaction: a reaction in which oxidation and reduction take place

reducing agent: a substance that reduces another substance during a redox reaction

oxidising agent: a substance that oxidises another substance during a redox reaction

electrolysis: the decomposition (breakdown) of an ionic compound when molten or in aqueous solution by the passage of an electric current

electrolyte: a compound which conducts electricity when molten or in solution in water and is decomposed in the process

anode: the positive electrode in an electrolytic cell

cathode: the negative electrode in an electrolytic cell

combustion: the burning of an element or compound in air or oxygen

displacement: a reaction in which a more reactive element displaces a less reactive element from a solution of a salt

USEFUL REACTIONS AND THEIR EQUATIONS

lead(II) bromide → lead + bromine

$PbBr_2 \rightarrow Pb + Br_2$ electrolysis

calcium carbonate → calcium oxide + carbon dioxide

$CaCO_3(s) \rightarrow CaO(s) + CO_2(g)$ thermal decomposition

magnesium + oxygen → magnesium oxide

$2Mg(s) + O_2(g) \rightarrow 2MgO(s)$ synthesis (oxidation)

copper oxide + hydrogen → copper + water

$CuO(s) + H_2(g) \rightarrow Cu(s) + H_2O(l)$ reduction

methane + oxygen → carbon dioxide + water

$CH_4(g) + O_2(g) \rightarrow CO_2(g) + 2H_2O(l)$ combustion

potassium iodide + chlorine → potassium chloride + iodine

$2KI(aq) + Cl_2(g) \rightarrow 2KCl(aq) + I_2(aq)$ displacement

copper(II) sulfate + zinc → zinc sulfate + copper

$CuSO_4(aq) + Zn(s) \rightarrow ZnSO_4(aq) + Cu(s)$ displacement

Exercise C5.1 The nature of electrolysis

This exercise will help you summarise the major aspects of electrolysis and its applications.

a Complete the following passage by using the words listed below.

anode	electrodes	current	molten	electrolyte	solution	cathode
positive	hydrogen	molecules	lose	oxygen		

Changes taking place during electrolysis

During electrolysis, ionic compounds are decomposed by the passage of an electric current. For this to happen, the compound must be either .... or in .... Electrolysis can occur when an electric .... passes through a molten .... The two rods dipping into the electrolyte are called the .... In this situation, metals are deposited at the .... and non-metals are formed at the ....

When the ionic compound is dissolved in water, the electrolysis can be more complex. Generally, during electrolysis .... ions move towards the .... and negative ions move towards the .... At the negative electrode (cathode) the metal or .... ions gain electrons and form metal atoms or hydrogen .... At the positive electrode (anode) certain non-metal ions .... electrons and .... or chlorine is produced.

b Complete the passage by using the words listed below.

hydrogen	hydroxide	lower	copper	sodium	molten
cryolite	purifying	positive	concentrated		

Examples of electrolysis in industry

There are several important industrial applications of electrolysis, the most important economically being the electrolysis of .... aluminium oxide to produce aluminium. The aluminium oxide is mixed with molten .... to .... the melting point of the electrolyte.

A .... aqueous solution of sodium chloride contains ...., chloride, hydrogen and .... ions. When this solution is electrolysed, ... rather than sodium is discharged at the negative electrode. The solution remaining is sodium hydroxide.

When a solution of copper(II) sulfate is electrolysed using .... electrodes, an unusual thing happens and the copper atoms of the .... electrode (anode) go into solution as copper ions. At the cathode the copper ions turn into copper atoms, and the metal is deposited on this electrode. This can be used as a method of refining or .... impure copper.

Exercise C5.2 Making and 'breaking' copper chloride

The difference between synthesis and decomposition is emphasised in this exercise together with a consideration of the energy changes involved.

'Dutch metal' is a form of brass containing a very high proportion of copper. It is generally used as very thin sheets for gilding, as imitation gold leaf.

Synthesising copper(II) chloride

a   What are the words we use to describe a metal that can be drawn out and beaten into thin sheets?

....

The following is a description of the reaction of Dutch metal with chlorine gas to produce copper(II) chloride.

A clean dry gas jar is filled with chlorine gas in a fume cupboard. The lid of the gas jar is lifted and two thin sheets of Dutch metal are lowered into the gas using tongs. The lid is quickly replaced.

A flash of flame is observed and clouds of yellow 'smoke' are formed.

A small volume of distilled water is added to the gas jar and shaken to dissolve the smoke. A pale blue-green (turquoise) solution is formed.

b   What colour is chlorine gas?

....

c   Why is the reaction carried out in a fume cupboard?

....

d   Is the reaction observed exothermic or endothermic? What feature of Dutch metal helps the reaction take place quickly? Explain your answers.

....

....

....

e   What observation indicates that the solution obtained contains copper(II) chloride?

....

f   Give the chemical equation for the synthesis reaction that has taken place.

....

g   Dutch metal is an alloy of copper (84%) and zinc (16%). What other salt may be present in the solution?

....

Decomposing copper(ɪɪ) chloride

Molten lead(II) bromide can be split into its elements by the passage of an electric current. The same is true for some salts when in aqueous solution. Here copper(II) chloride can be decomposed to its elements by electrolysis. A simple cell such as the one shown here can be set up so that the chlorine gas can be collected.

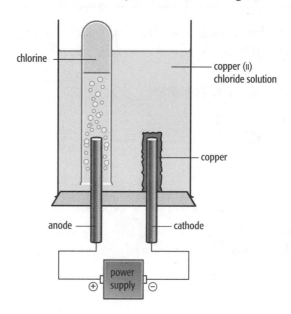

a   Write word and symbol equations for the overall reaction taking place during this electrolysis.

....

....

b   Define the term **electrolysis**.

....

....

....

....

c   How would you test the gas collected at the anode to show that it was chlorine?

....

....

d A much simpler set of apparatus can be used to show this electrolysis. This is shown below.

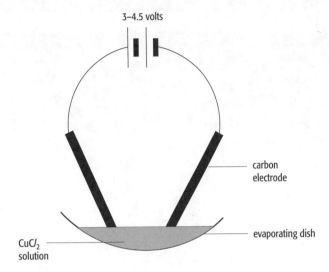

i If this simpler apparatus is used, where must the electrolysis be carried out for safety reasons?

....

ii Using this simple apparatus, there is no collection of any gas produced. How could you test to show that chlorine had been produced in this case? Explain why it would work.

....

....

....

e Is the decomposition of copper(II) chloride exothermic or endothermic? What type of energy is involved in this reaction?

....

....

f Write the half-equations for the reactions taking place at the anode (positive electrode) and the cathode (negative electrode). Use your knowledge of the half-equations for the electrolysis of molten lead(II) bromide to help here, but be careful of the state symbols.

At the anode:

....

At the cathode:

....

DEFINITIONS TO LEARN

exothermic reaction: a reaction that gives out heat to the surroundings

endothermic reaction: a reaction that takes in heat from the surroundings

photochemical reaction: a reaction that requires light in order to happen

rate of reaction: the rate of formation of the products of a chemical reaction (or the rate at which the reactants are used up)

catalyst: a substance that speeds up a chemical reaction but remains unchanged at the end of the reaction

enzyme: a protein that functions as a biological catalyst

reversible reaction: a chemical reaction which can go both forwards and backwards; the symbol $\rightleftharpoons$ is used in the equation for the reaction

activation energy: the minimum amount of energy the reacting molecules must have for a reaction to take place

equilibrium: a position which arises when both the forward and reverse reactions of a reversible reaction are taking place at the same speed – there is then no change in the concentration of the reactants and products unless the physical conditions are changed

USEFUL REACTIONS AND THEIR EQUATIONS

These reactions are often used to study reaction rates or are useful examples of reversible reactions:

$Mg + 2HCl \rightarrow MgCl_2 + H_2$

$CaCO_3 + 2HCl \rightarrow CaCl_2 + H_2O + CO_2$

$CuSO_4 + 5H_2O \rightleftharpoons CuSO_4 \cdot 5H_2O$

$N_2 + 3H_2 \rightleftharpoons 2NH_3$

$2H_2O_2(l) \rightarrow 2H_2O(l) + O_2(g)$

$Na_2S_2O_3(aq) + 2HCl(aq) \rightarrow 2NaCl(aq) + SO_2(g) + H_2O(l) + S(s)$

$2SO_2(g) + O_2(g) \rightleftharpoons 2SO_3(g)$

Exercise C6.1 Energy diagrams

This exercise is aimed at helping you understand energy level diagrams and their usefulness in showing why some reactions are exothermic while others are endothermic.

The energy changes involved in chemical reactions can be represented visually by energy level diagrams. Such diagrams show the relative stability of the reactants and products. The more stable a set of reactants or products, the lower their energy level.

The energy level diagram for an exothermic reaction is different from that for an endothermic reaction. The following keywords/phrases will be needed to fill in the information boxes accompanying the diagrams.

| given out | positive | taken in | reactants | negative | products |

a Exothermic reactions

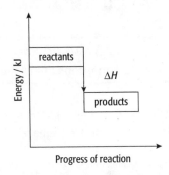

Use information from the diagram and the keywords/phrases to complete the following information box.

In an exothermic reaction, the .... have more energy than

the ....

This means that ΔH is ....

The difference in energy is .... as heat.

The temperature of the surroundings **increases/decreases**. (*Delete the incorrect word.*)

b Endothermic reactions

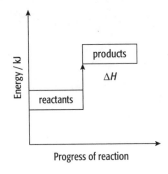

Again, use information from the diagram and the keywords/phrases to complete the following information box.

In an endothermic reaction, the .... have more energy

than the ....

This means that ΔH is ....

The difference in energy is .... from the surroundings.

The temperature of the surroundings **increases/decreases**. (*Delete the incorrect word.*)

Exercise C6.2 The collision theory of reaction rates

This exercise should help you develop an understanding of the collision (particle) theory of reactions and how changing conditions affect the rate of various types of reaction.

Complete the following table from your understanding of the factors that affect the speed (rate) of a reaction. Several of the sections have been completed already. The finished table should then be a useful revision aid.

Factor affecting the reaction	Types of reaction affected	Change made in the condition	Effect on rate of reaction
concentration	all reactions involving solutions or reactions involving gases	an increase in the concentration of one, or both, of the .... means there are more particles in the same volume	increases the rate of reaction as the particles .... more frequently
pressure	reactions involving .... only	an increase in the pressure	greatly .... the rate of reaction – the effect is the same as that of an increase in ....
temperature	all reactions	an increase in temperature – this means that molecules are moving .... and collide more ....; the particles also have more .... when they collide	.... the rate of reaction

(Continued)

38

Factor affecting the reaction	Types of reaction affected	Change made in the condition	Effect on rate of reaction
particle size	reactions involving solids and liquids, solids and gases or mixtures of solids	use the same mass of a solid but make the pieces of solid	greatly increases the rate of reaction
light	a number photochemical reactions including photosynthesis, the reaction between methane and chlorine, and the reaction on photographic film	reaction in the presence of .... or UV light	greatly increases the rate of reaction
using a catalyst	slow reactions can be speeded up by adding a suitable catalyst	reduces amount of .... required for the reaction to take place: the catalyst is present in the same .... at the end of the reaction	.... the rate of reaction

Exercise C6.3 The influence of surface area on the rate of reaction

> **This exercise should help develop your skills in presenting and manipulating experimental data. You will also be asked to interpret data and draw conclusions from it.**

A useful experiment that shows the effect of varying the surface area of a solid on reaction rate is based on the fact that hydrochloric acid reacts with calcium carbonate to produce the gas carbon dioxide.

The experiment was set up as shown below using identical masses of marble chips. Flask **A** contains larger pieces of marble chips and Flask **B** contains smaller pieces. The same concentration and volume of acid was used in both flasks.

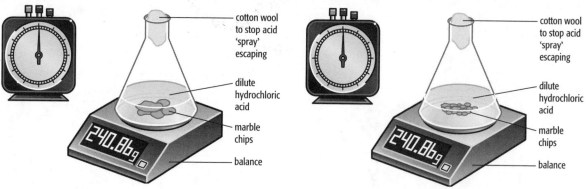

Flask **A**: larger pieces of marble chips

Flask **B**: smaller pieces of marble chips

The flasks were quickly and simultaneously set to zero on the balances. The mass loss of the flasks was then recorded over time.

a Write the word equation for the reaction between marble chips (calcium carbonate) and dilute hydrochloric acid.

....

b What causes the loss in mass from the flasks?

....

....

Readings on the digital balance were taken every 30 seconds. The balance had been tared (set) to zero at the start of the reaction.

For the large pieces of marble chips (Flask **A**), readings (in g) were:

 0.00 −0.21 −0.46 −0.65 −0.76 −0.81 −0.91

−0.92 −0.96 −0.98 −0.98 −1.00 −0.99 −0.99

For the small pieces of marble chips (Flask **B**), readings (in g) were:

 0.00 −0.51 −0.78 −0.87 −0.91 −0.94 −0.96

−0.98 −0.99 −0.99 −0.99 −1.00 −0.99 −1.00

c Create a suitable table showing how the mass of carbon dioxide produced (equal to the loss of mass) varies with time for the two experiments.

d Plot the **two** graphs on the grid.

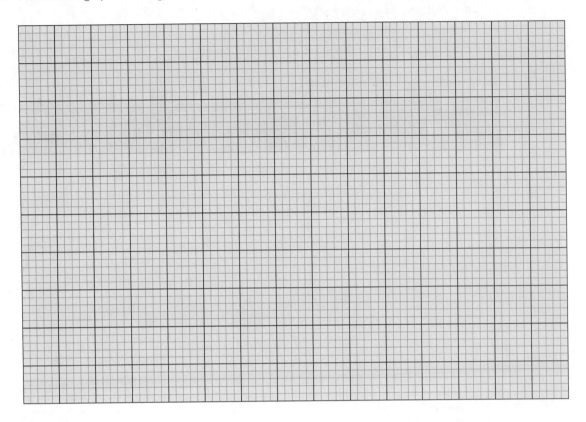

e Which pieces gave the faster rate of reaction? Explain why.

....

....

....

f Explain why, for both flasks, the same amount of gas is produced in the end.

....

....

....

Use the checklist below to give yourself a mark for your graph. For each point, award yourself:

- 2 marks if you did it really well
- 1 mark if you made a good attempt at it, and partly succeeded
- 0 marks if you did not try to do it, or did not succeed.

Self-assessment checklist for graphs:

Check point	Marks awarded	
	You	Your teacher
You have drawn the axes with a ruler, using most of the width and height of the grid.		
You have used a good scale for the *x*-axis and the *y*-axis, going up in 0.25 s, 0.5 s, 1 s or 2 s.		
You have labelled the axes correctly, giving the correct units for the scales on both axes.		
You have plotted each point precisely and correctly.		
You have used a small, neat cross or dot for each point.		
You have drawn a single, clear best-fit line through each set of points.		
You have ignored any anomalous results when drawing the line through each set of points.		
Total (out of 14)		

12–14   Excellent.

10–11   Good.

7–9   A good start, but you need to improve quite a bit.

5–6   Poor. Try this same graph again, using a new sheet of graph paper.

1–4   Very poor. Read through all the criteria again, and then try the same graph again.

Exercise C6.4 Finding the rate of a reaction producing a gas

This exercise is based on an important practical technique of gas collection using a gas syringe. Following through the exercise should help develop your skills in presenting experimental data and calculating results from it. You will also be asked how the experiment could be modified to provide further data.

Hydrogen peroxide, H_2O_2, is an unstable compound that decomposes slowly at room temperature to form water and oxygen.

$$2H_2O_2(aq) \rightarrow 2H_2O(l) + O_2(g)$$

A student investigated how the rate of decomposition depends on the catalyst. She tested two catalysts: manganese(IV) oxide (experiment **1**) and copper (experiment **2**). The volume of oxygen produced by the reaction was measured at different times using the apparatus shown.

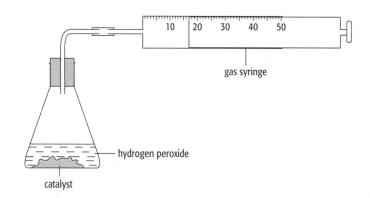

gas syringe

hydrogen peroxide

catalyst

a Use the data from the diagrams below to complete the results for experiment **2** in the following table.

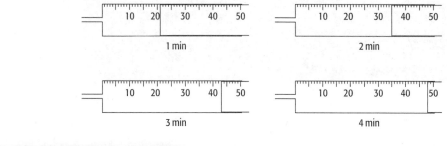

1 min

2 min

3 min

4 min

Time / min	1	2	3	4	5	6
Volume of oxygen collected in experiment 1 / cm³	9	17	24	29	32	35
Volume of oxygen collected in experiment 2 / cm³	....	....	....	....	50	50

b Plot the results from experiments **1** and **2** on the grid and draw a smooth curve through each set of points. Label the curves you draw as **exp.1** and **exp.2**.

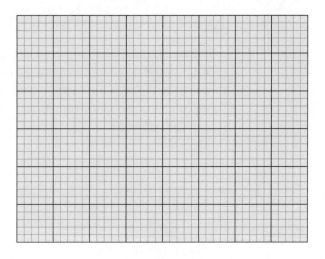

c Which of the two experiments was the first to reach completion? Explain your answer.

....

....

....

d Use your graph to estimate the time taken in experiment **1** to double the volume of oxygen produced from 15 cm³ to 30 cm³. Record your answers in the table, and indicate on the graph how you obtained your values.

Time taken to produce 30 cm³ / min	....
Time taken to produce 15 cm³ / min	....
Time taken to double the volume from 15 cm³ to 30 cm³ / min	....

Experiment 1 (using manganese(ıv) oxide)

e The rate (or speed) of a reaction may be calculated using the formula:

$$\text{rate of reaction} = \frac{\text{volume of oxygen produced / cm}^3}{\text{time taken / mim}}$$

Using the two graphs and the above formula, calculate the rate of each reaction after the first 2.5 min for each experiment.

f   From your answer to **e**, suggest which is the better catalyst, manganese(IV) oxide or copper. Explain your answer.

....

....

g   At the end of experiment **2** the copper was removed from the solution by filtration. It was dried and weighed. How would you predict this mass of copper would compare with the mass of copper added at the start of the experiment? Explain your answer.

....

....

h   Suggest how the rate of decomposition in either experiment could be further increased.

....

....

....

DEFINITIONS TO LEARN

acid: a substance that dissolves in water to give a solution with a pH below 7

base: a substance which will neutralise an acid to give a salt and water only

alkali: a base that dissolves in water

pH scale: a measure of the acidity or alkalinity of a solution (scale from 0 to 14)

indicator: a substance that changes colour depending on whether it is in an acid or alkali

salt: an ionic substance produced from an acid by neutralisation with a base

neutralisation reaction: a reaction between an acid and a base to produce a salt and water only

limewater: a solution of calcium hydroxide, $Ca(OH)_2(aq)$, used as the analytical test for carbon dioxide

USEFUL REACTIONS AND THEIR EQUATIONS

Neutralisation reactions

$HCl(aq) + NaOH(aq) \rightarrow NaCl(aq) + H_2O(l)$

$H_2SO_4(aq) + 2KOH(aq) \rightarrow K_2SO_4(aq) + 2H_2O(l)$

$HNO_3(aq) + NH_3(aq) \rightarrow NH_4NO_3(aq)$

$CuO(s) + H_2SO_4(aq) \rightarrow CuSO_4(aq) + H_2O(l)$

Other characteristic acid reactions

$CaCO_3(s) + 2HCl(aq) \rightarrow CaCl_2(aq) + CO_2(g) + H_2O(l)$

$CuCO_3(s) + H_2SO_4(aq) \rightarrow CuSO_4(aq) + CO_2(g) + H_2O(l)$

$Zn(s) + H_2SO_4(aq) \rightarrow ZnSO_4(aq) + H_2(g)$

$Mg(s) + 2HCl(aq) \rightarrow MgCl_2(aq) + H_2(g)$

Precipitation reactions

$FeSO_4(aq) + 2NaOH(aq) \rightarrow Fe(OH)_2(s) + Na_2SO_4(aq)$

$AlCl_3(aq) + 3NaOH(aq) \rightarrow Al(OH)_3(s) + 3NaCl(aq)$

$AgNO_3(aq) + KI(aq) \rightarrow AgI(s) + KNO_3(aq)$

$CO_2(g) + Ca(OH)_2 \rightarrow CaCO_3(s) + H_2O(l)$

Exercise C7.1 Acid and base reactions – neutralisation

This exercise will help you familiarise yourself with some of the terms involved in talking about acids and bases.

Choose words from the list below to fill in the gaps in the following statements.

acid	carbon dioxide	hydrogen	hydrated	anhydrous
metal	precipitation	sodium	sulfuric	water

All salts are **ionic** compounds. Salts are produced when an alkali neutralises an ....

In this reaction, the salt is formed when a .... ion or an ammonium ion from the alkali

replaces one or more .... ions of the acid.

Salts can be crystallised from the solution produced by the neutralisation reaction. The salt crystals formed often contain .... of crystallisation. These salts are called .... salts. The salt crystals can be heated to drive off the .... of crystallisation. The salt remaining is said to be ....

Salts can be made by other reactions of acids. Magnesium sulfate can be made by reacting magnesium carbonate with .... acid. The gas given off is .... Water is also formed in this reaction.

All .... salts are soluble in water. Insoluble salts are usually prepared by ....

Exercise C7.2 Types of salt

This exercise aims to increase your confidence in predicting the products of the characteristic reactions of acids, particularly in terms of naming the salt produced in a reaction.

Salts are produced in reactions where the hydrogen of an acid is replaced by metal ions or the ammonium ion. Each acid gives a characteristic family of salts. Sulfuric acid, for instance, always produces sulfates.

a Complete the following statements for other acids.

  i Hydrochloric acid always produces ....

  ii Nitric acid always produces ....

  iii Ethanoic acid always produces ....

  iv Phosphoric acid always produces ....

b Complete the table below which summarises the products of various reactions of acids.

Substances reacted together		Salt produced	Other products of the reaction
dilute hydrochloric acid	zinc oxide	....	....
dilute sulfuric acid	....	copper sulfate	water and carbon dioxide
....	....	magnesium sulfate	water and carbon dioxide
....	....	magnesium chloride	hydrogen
dilute nitric acid	copper oxide	....	....
dilute ethanoic acid	....	sodium ethanoate	water
....	potassium hydroxide	potassium phosphate	....

Exercise C7.3 Descaling a coffee machine

The formation of limescale in coffee makers, kettles and hot water pipes is a problem in certain areas. This exercise considers various acids that are used to remove limescale and their effectiveness.

Coffee makers can become blocked with 'limescale' in hard water areas. Limescale is calcium carbonate which precipitates from the hot water in the machine and blocks the pipes.

It is often necessary to 'descale' the machines. This is done by passing acid through the pipes. The acid reacts with the calcium carbonate and so removes it.

The following acids have been used for descaling:

- hydrochloric acid
- citric acid
- ethanoic acid (vinegar)
- sulfamic acid.

a Write word and symbol equations for the reaction between calcium carbonate and hydrochloric acid.

....

....

b What name would be given to the salt formed when citric acid reacts with calcium carbonate?

....

c Why might these acids not be the best to use for descaling a coffee machine?

i Hydrochloric acid

....

ii Ethanoic acid

....

d Search the internet to find the answers to the following questions.

i What is the formula of sulfamic acid and what is it used for?

....

....

ii Why does water sometimes produce calcium carbonate (limescale) when it is heated? What is hard water?

....

....

....

....

....

Exercise C7.4 Thermochemistry – investigating the neutralisation of an acid by an alkali

> This exercise introduces an unfamiliar form of titration and further develops your skills in presenting, processing and evaluating the results of practical work.

The reaction between dilute nitric acid and dilute sodium hydroxide solutions can be investigated by thermochemistry. This can be done by following the changes in temperature as one solution is added to another.

Apparatus

- polystyrene cup and beaker
- 25 cm³ measuring cylinder
- 100 cm³ measuring cylinder
- thermometer (0 to 100 °C)
- **safety glasses – to be used when handling the acid and alkali solutions**

Method

An experiment was carried out to measure the temperature changes during the neutralisation of sodium hydroxide solution with dilute nitric acid. Both solutions were allowed to stand in the laboratory for about 30 minutes.

25 cm³ of sodium hydroxide solution was added to a polystyrene beaker and the temperature was measured. Then 10 cm³ of nitric acid was added to the alkali in the beaker and the highest temperature reached was measured. The experiment was repeated using the following volumes of acid: 20, 30, 40, 50 and 60 cm³.

Results

Temperature of alkali solution at start of experiment = 21.0 °C.

The following temperatures were obtained for the different volumes of added acid used:

28.0, 35.0, 35.0, 31.0, 30.0 and 27.5 °C respectively.

a Record these results in a suitable table.

Use this checklist to give yourself a mark for your results table. For each point, award yourself:

- 2 marks if you did it really well
- 1 mark if you made a good attempt at it, and partly succeeded
- 0 marks if you did not try to do it, or did not succeed.

Self-assessment checklist for results tables:

Check point	Marks awarded	
	You	Your teacher
You have drawn the table with a ruler.		
The headings are appropriate and have the correct units in each column/row.		
The table is easy for someone else to read and understand.		
If the table contains readings, all are to the same number of decimal places (for example 15.5, 14.2, etc).		
Total (out of 8)		

8   Excellent.

7   Good.

5–6   A good start, but you need to improve quite a bit.

3–4   Poor. Try this same results table again, using a new sheet of paper.

1–2   Very poor. Read through all the criteria again, and then try the same results table again.

b   Plot a graph of the temperature of the solution against the volume of acid added to the alkali.

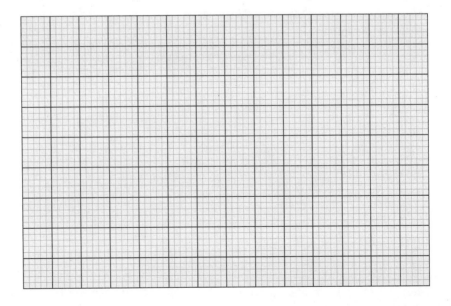

c Draw suitable lines through the points on your graph. (Note that there are two parts to this graph so you will need to draw **two** straight lines through the points and extend them until they cross.)

d Which point appears to be inaccurate?

....

e From these results work out the volume of acid needed to neutralise 25 cm³ of the sodium hydroxide solution. Explain why you have chosen this value.

....

....

Use the checklist below to give yourself a mark for your graph. For each point, award yourself:
- **2 marks if you did it really well**
- **1 mark if you made a good attempt at it, and partly succeeded**
- **0 marks if you did not try to do it, or did not succeed.**

Self-assessment checklist for graphs:

Check point	Marks awarded	
	You	**Your teacher**
You have drawn the axes with a ruler, using most of the width and height of the grid.		
You have used a good scale for the *x*-axis and the *y*-axis, going up in 1 s, 2 s, 5 s or 10 s.		
You have labelled the axes correctly, giving the correct units for the scales on both axes.		
You have plotted each point precisely and correctly.		
You have used a small, neat cross for each point.		
You have drawn a single, clear best-fit line through each set of points – using a ruler for straight lines – and have extended the lines to meet.		
You have ignored any anomalous results when drawing the lines.		
Total (out of 14)		

12–14 Excellent.

10–11 Good.

7–9 A good start, but you need to improve quite a bit.

5–6 Poor. Try this same graph again, using a new sheet of graph paper.

1–4 Very poor. Read through all the criteria again, and then try the same graph again.

f Why were the solutions left to stand for about 30 minutes before the experiments?

....

g Why was a polystyrene beaker used instead of a glass beaker?

....

h Suggest **three** improvements that would make the experiment more accurate.

....

....

....

i Write the word equation and balanced chemical equation for the reaction.

....

....

j Is the reaction exothermic or endothermic?

....

k The concentration of the sodium hydroxide solution is 1.0 mole per dm^3. How many moles are there in 25 cm^3 of this solution? (Remember there are 1000 cm^3 in 1 dm^3.)

....

l Look at the equation and work out how many moles of nitric acid this would react with.

....

m Calculate how many moles of acid there are in 1000 cm^3 of the acid solution. What is the concentration of the acid solution in moles per dm^3?

....

DEFINITION TO LEARN

alkali metal: a reactive metal in Group I of the Periodic Table; alkali metals react with water to produce alkaline solutions

a halogen: a reactive non-metallic element in Group VII of the Periodic Table

a noble gas: an unreactive monoatomic gas in Group VIII (or 0) of the Periodic Table

 USEFUL REACTIONS AND THEIR EQUATIONS

$2Na + 2H_2O \rightarrow 2NaOH + H_2$

$Fe_2O_3 + 2Al \rightarrow Al_2O_3 + 2Fe$

$Zn(s) + CuSO_4(aq) \rightarrow ZnSO_4(aq) + Cu(s)$

$CaCO_3(s) \rightarrow CaO(s) + CO_2(g)$

$2Cu(NO_3)_2(s) \rightarrow 2CuO(s) + 4NO_2(g) + O_2(g)$

Exercise C8.1   Trends in the halogens

This exercise examines the trends in physical properties of elements within a non-metal group of the Periodic Table. It should help you develop your skills at analysing and predicting trends within a group.

The table shows some of the physical properties of the elements of Group VII at atmospheric pressure. These elements are known as the halogens and the properties show distinct trends as you go down the group.

Element	Proton number	Melting point/°C	Boiling point/°C	Colour
fluorine	9	−219	−188	pale yellow
chlorine	17	−101	−34	pale green
bromine	35	−6		
iodine	53	114	185	grey-black
astatine	85	303	337	

a Plot a graph of the melting points and boiling points of the halogens against their proton numbers. Join the points for each property together to produce two separate lines on the graph.

Draw a line across the graph at 20 °C (room temperature) to help you decide which elements are solid, liquid or gas at room temperature and pressure.

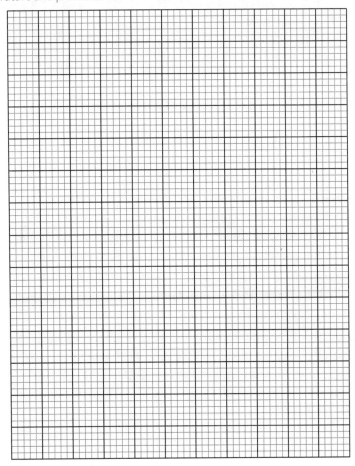

b Use your graph to estimate the boiling point of bromine, and state its colour and physical state at room temperature.

Estimated boiling point:............................ °C   Colour:..

Physical state:...

c Which of the halogens are gases at room temperature and pressure?

....

d Astatine is very rarely seen. What would you predict to be its physical state and colour at room temperature and pressure?

....

e What is the trend observed in the melting points of the halogens as you go down the group?

....

Exercise C8.2 Displacement reactions of the halogens

This exercise will build your understanding of a certain type of reaction and help improve your skills in organising and presenting experimental observations.

The halogens – chlorine, bromine and iodine – differ in terms of their ability to displace another halogen from a solution of its salt. The following are some notes from a students experiment. They include some rough observations from the tests carried out.

The halogens were provided as solutions in water and the test was to add the halogen to the salt solution. Solutions of potassium chloride, potassium bromide and potassium iodide were provided.

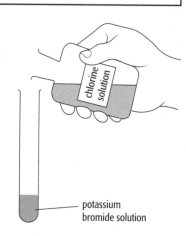

chlorine solution

potassium bromide solution

To add further observations, hexane was also available as a solvent to mix with the reaction mixture at the end of the experiment. If there appeared to be a reaction, the product was shaken with hexane and the layers allowed to separate. The colour, if any, of the hexane layer was noted.

Results

1 *Rough notes: KCl solution with bromine or iodine solutions – no change to colourless solution – hexane not added.*
2 *KBr solution with iodine solution – no change to colourless solution – hexane not added.*
3 *KBr solution with chlorine solution – solution colourless to brown – brown colour moves to upper hexane layer at end.*
4 *KI solution with chlorine or bromine water – solution colourless to brown in both cases – purple colour in upper hexane layer at end (brown colour of aqueous layer reduced).*

a Take these recorded observations and draw up a table of the results. If there is no change, then write 'no reaction'.

Use this checklist to give yourself a mark for your results table. For each point, award yourself:

- 2 marks if you did it really well
- 1 mark if you made a good attempt at it, and partly succeeded
- 0 marks if you did not try to do it, or did not succeed.

Self-assessment checklist for results tables:

Check point	Marks awarded	
	You	Your teacher
You have drawn the table with a ruler.		
The headings are appropriate and cover the observations you expect to make.		
The observations are recorded accurately, clearly and concisely – without over-elaboration.		
The table is easy for someone else to read and understand.		
Total (out of 8)		

8	Excellent.
7	Good.
5–6	A good start, but you need to improve quite a bit.
3–4	Poor. Try this same results table again, using a new sheet of paper.
1–2	Very poor. Read through all the criteria again, and then try the same results table again.

b Use the results to complete the diagram below which places the halogens tested in order of increasing reactivity.

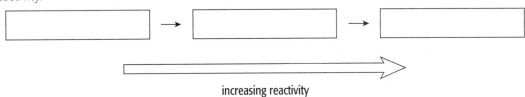

increasing reactivity

Exercise C8.3 Group I: The alkali metals

> This exercise should help you learn certain key properties of the alkali metals, and help develop the skills of predicting the properties of unfamiliar elements from the features of those that you have learnt.

Caesium is an alkali metal. It is in Group I of the Periodic Table.

a State **two** physical properties of caesium.

....

....

b State the number of electrons in the outer shell of a caesium atom. ....

c Complete the table below to estimate the boiling point and atomic radius of caesium. Comment also on the reactivity of potassium and caesium with water.

Group I metal	Density / g / cm³	Radius of metal atom / nm	Boiling point / °C	Reactivity with water
sodium	0.97	0.191	883	floats and fizzes quickly on the surface, disappears gradually and does not burst into flame
potassium	0.86	0.235	760	....
rubidium	1.53	0.250	686	reacts instantaneously, fizzes and bursts into flame then spits violently and may explode
caesium	1.88	....	....	....

d Write the word equation for the reaction of caesium with water.

....

DEFINITIONS TO LEARN

transition metal: a metal in the central block of the Periodic Table; transition metals are hard, dense metals that form coloured compounds and can have more than one valency

reactivity series: a listing of the metals in order of their reactivity

alloys: are mixtures of metals with other elements; examples include brass (copper and zinc) and mild steel (iron and carbon)

USEFUL REACTIONS AND THEIR EQUATIONS

$2K + 2H_2O \rightarrow 2KOH + H_2$

$Fe_2O_3 + 2Al \rightarrow Al_2O_3 + 2Fe$

$Mg(s) + CuSO_4(aq) \rightarrow MgSO_4(aq) + Cu(s)$

$CuCO_3(s) \rightarrow CuO(s) + CO_2(g)$

$2Pb(NO_3)_2(s) \rightarrow 2PbO(s) + 4NO_2(g) + O_2(g)$

Exercise C9.1 The reactivity series of metals

> This exercise should help you familiarise yourself with certain aspects of the reactivity series. It should also help develop your skills in interpreting practical observations and predicting the properties of unfamiliar elements from the features of those that you have learnt.

Using the results of various different types of chemical reaction, the metals can be arranged into the reactivity series.

a   Magnesium reacts very slowly indeed with cold water but it does react strongly with steam to give magnesium oxide and a gas. Write the word equation for the reaction between magnesium and steam.

....

b   Choose **one** metal from the reactivity series that will not react with steam.

....

c   Choose **one** metal from the reactivity series that will safely react with dilute sulfuric acid.

....

d In each of the experiments below, a piece of metal is placed in a solution of a metal salt. Complete the table of observations.

		zinc — iron(II) sulfate solution	zinc — copper(II) sulfate solution	iron — copper(II) sulfate solution	silver — copper(II) sulfate solution	copper — silver nitrate solution
At start	colour of metal	grey	....	silver-coloured	silver-coloured	....
At start	colour of solution	pale green	....	blue	blue	colourless
At finish	colour of metal	coated with metallic crystals	....	coated with brown solid	silver-coloured	coated with silver-coloured crystals
At finish	colour of solution	colourless	....	pale green	blue	....

e Use these results to place the metals **copper**, **iron**, **silver** and **zinc** in order of reactivity (putting the most reactive metal first).

.... > .... > .... > ....

The reactivity series of metals given in the box contains both familiar and unfamiliar elements. The unfamiliar elements are marked with an asterisk (*) and their common oxidation states are given. Choose metal(s) from this list to answer the following questions.

barium*	Ba (+2)
lanthanum*	La (+3)
aluminium	
zinc	
chromium*	Cr (+2),(+3),(+6)
iron	
copper	
palladium*	Pd (+2)

f Which **two** metals would not react with dilute hydrochloric acid?

....

g   Which **two** unfamiliar metals would react with cold water?

....

h   Name an unfamiliar metal that could not be extracted from its oxide by reduction with carbon.

....

i   Why should you be able to predict that metals such as iron and chromium have more than one oxidation state?

....

Exercise C9.2   Energy from displacement reactions

This exercise will help you practise the presentation and interpretation of practical experiments.

When a metal is added to a solution of the salt of a less reactive metal, a displacement reaction takes place. The equations for two different examples are:

$$Fe(s) + CuSO_4(aq) \rightarrow Cu(s) + FeSO_4(aq)$$
zinc + copper sulfate → copper + zinc sulfate

The energy change involved in these reactions can be measured by adding 5 g of metal powder to 50 cm³ of 0.5 mol/dm³ copper (II) sulfate solution in a polystyrene cup. The temperature of the solution is taken before adding the metal. The powder is then added, the reaction mixture is stirred continuously, and temperatures are taken every 30 seconds for 3 minutes.

A student took the readings that follow when carrying out this experiment.

Time / min	0.0	0.5	1.0	1.5	2.0	2.5	3.0
Experiment 1 (zinc): temperature / °C	21	48	62	71	75	72	70
Experiment 2 (iron): temperature / °C	21	25	32	38	41	43	44

a Plot **two** graphs on the grid provided and label each with the name of the metal.

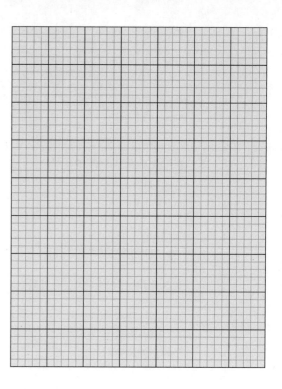

b Write the word equation for the first reaction and the balanced symbol equation for the second.

....

....

c Which metal, iron or zinc, produced the larger temperature rise?

....

d Suggest why this metal gave the larger temperature rise.

....

....

e Comment on whether this experiment is a 'fair test'. Explain your answer.

....

....

....

Use the checklist below to give yourself a mark for your graph. For each point, award yourself:

- **2 marks** if you did it really well
- **1 mark** if you made a good attempt at it, and partly succeeded
- **0 marks** if you did not try to do it, or did not succeed.

Self-assessment checklist for graphs:

Check point	Marks awarded	
	You	Your teacher
You have drawn the axes with a ruler, using most of the width and height of the grid.		
You have used a good scale for the *x*-axis and the *y*-axis, going up in useful proportions.		
You have labelled the axes correctly, giving the correct units for the scales on both axes.		
You have plotted each point precisely and correctly.		
You have used a small, neat dot or cross for each point.		
You have drawn a single, clear best-fit line through each set of points – using a ruler for a straight line.		
You have ignored any anomalous results when drawing the lines through each set of results.		
Total (out of 14)		

12–14   Excellent.

10–11   Good.

7–9   A good start, but you need to improve quite a bit.

5–6   Poor. Try this same graph again, using a new sheet of graph paper.

1–4   Very poor. Read through all the criteria again, and then try the same graph again.

Exercise C9.3 Metals and alloys

This exercise discusses some aspects of alloys and their usefulness. It explores the advantages and specific purpose of certain alloys.

The table shows some properties of a selection of pure metals.

Metal	Relative abundance in Earth's crust	Cost of extraction	Density	Strength	Melting point / °C	Electrical conductivity relative to iron
iron	2nd	low	high	high	1535	1.0
titanium	7th	very high	low	high	1660	0.2
aluminium	1st	high	low	medium	660	3.5
zinc	19th	low	high	low	419	1.7
copper	20th	low	high	medium	1083	6.0
tin	40th	low	high	low	231	0.9
lead	30th	low	very high	low	327	0.5

Use information from the table to answer the following questions.

a   Why is aluminium used for overhead power cables?

....

b   Why do the aluminium cables have an iron (or steel) core?

....

c   Why is copper used instead of aluminium in wiring in the home?

....

d   Why is titanium a good metal to use for jet aircraft and Formula 1 racing cars?

....

....

Alloys have different properties from the metals they are made from. They are usually harder and stronger with lower melting points.

e **Solder**, which is melted to join together electrical components on circuit boards, is a mixture of tin and lead. Suggest why it is used in preference to the pure metals.

....

....

f **Brass** is an alloy of copper and zinc. It is used to make brass musical instruments and to make electrical connectors and plugs.

There are two main types of brass: 60 : 40 and 70 : 30 copper to zinc. The larger the amount of zinc, the harder and stronger the alloy is.

Suggest which alloy is used for each of the purposes mentioned above. Give a reason for your answers.

Cu60 : Zn40

....

....

Cu70 : Zn30

....

....

65

🔑 **DEFINITIONS TO LEARN**

acid rain: rainfall with a pH usually less than 5 resulting from dissolved atmospheric pollution

greenhouse gas: a gas which absorbs heat (infrared radiation) and keeps the surface of the planet warm

photosynthesis: the photochemical reaction in the green leaves of plants that turns carbon dioxide and water into glucose and oxygen

respiration: the biochemical reaction in living cells that produces energy from the reaction of glucose and oxygen to produce carbon dioxide and water

🔑 **USEFUL REACTIONS AND THEIR EQUATIONS**

carbon dioxide + water → glucose + oxygen	$6CO_2 + 6H_2O \rightarrow C_6H_{12}O_6 + 6O_2$	photosynthesis
glucose + oxygen → carbon dioxide + water	$C_6H_{12}O_6 + 6O_2 \rightarrow 6CO_2 + 6H_2O$	respiration

Exercise C10.1 Atmospheric pollution, industry and transport

This exercise discusses different aspects of atmospheric pollution and relates it to key aspects of human activity. It will help you in developing your skills in evaluating data and drawing conclusions from them.

The following pie charts show estimates of the sources of three major atmospheric pollutants in an industrialised country.

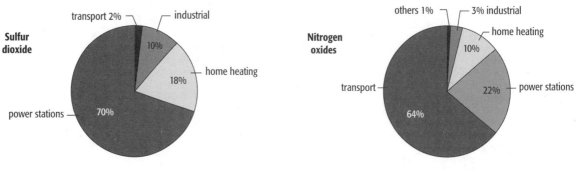

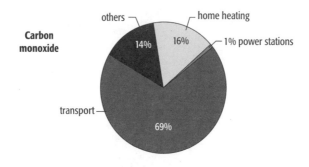

a What is the largest source of sulfur dioxide pollution?

....

b Name the **three** major fuels whose combustion gives rise to the levels of sulfur dioxide in the atmosphere.

....

c Units are being added to the some power stations and industrial plants to prevent the emission of sulfur dioxide. What is the name given to these units?

....

d Nitrogen oxides (NO_x) are another major pollutant of the atmosphere, particularly in large cities.

i Nitrogen monoxide is formed by the reaction of nitrogen and oxygen inside the hot engine of cars and other vehicles. Complete the following equation for the reaction producing nitrogen monoxide.

$$N_2 + O_2 \rightarrow \text{......} NO$$

ii When leaving the car, nitrogen monoxide in the exhaust fumes reacts further with oxygen in the air to produce the brown gas which can be seen in the atmosphere over large cities. This gas is nitrogen dioxide. Balance the equation for the production of this gas.

nitrogen monoxide + oxygen → nitrogen dioxide

$$\text{......} NO \quad + \quad O_2 \quad \rightarrow \quad \text{......} NO_2$$

iii The operating temperature of a diesel engine is significantly higher than that of a petrol (gasoline) engine. Would you expect the level of NO_x emissions from a diesel-powered vehicle to be greater or lower than from a petrol-powered vehicle? Give the reason for your answer.

....

....

iv What attachment is fitted to modern cars to reduce the level of pollution by oxides of nitrogen?

....

e Nitrogen oxides, unburnt hydrocarbons and carbon monoxide combine together under the influence of ultraviolet light to produce photochemical smog.

    i Why do you think this form of pollution is most common in large cities?

    ....

    ....

    ii What other form of pollution from car exhaust fumes has now almost totally disappeared from modern cities following changes in fuel and pollution monitoring?

    ....

f In order to control traffic flow, the city of London in the United Kingdom introduced a 'congestion charge' for vehicles entering the centre of the city in 2003. The table shows figures for the percentage fall in the levels of certain pollutants following the introduction of the congestion charge.

	Pollutant gas within Congestion Charge Zone	
	NO_x	CO_2
Overall traffic emissions change 2003 versus 2002 / %	−13.4	−16.4
Overall traffic emissions change 2004 versus 2003 / %	−5.2	−0.9
Change due to improved vehicle technology, 2003 to 2006 / %	−17.3	−3.4

    i What was the measured percentage drop in the level of nitrogen oxides within the Congestion Charge Zone over the first two years following the introduction of the charge?

    ....

    ....

    ....

    ii At face value there seems to be a drop in the levels of pollutants following the introduction of the congestion charge. But should we expect the fall in pollution levels to continue?

    ....

    ....

    iii An independent study published in 2011 suggested that other factors should be taken into account, particularly when trying to study a relatively small area within a large city. One factor is hinted at in the third row of figures. What is that factor; and what other influences need to be taken into account in considering this situation?

    ....

    ....

    ....

    ....

g The use of fossil fuels in industry and transport also produces carbon dioxide. What is the reasoning behind the slogan painted on these freight containers seen waiting to be loaded on to a freight train outside a major UK station? Outline the argument behind the slogan.

....

....

....

....

....

....

Exercise C10.2 Clean water is crucial

This exercise covers aspects of how we produce clean water for domestic and industrial use, focusing on stages that depend on key physical and chemical techniques.

The provision of clean drinking water and sanitation to more of the world's population is one of the key millennium goals of the United Nations. The lack of this basic provision impacts not only on the levels of disease in an area, in particular the mortality rate of children, but also on the level of education and the role of women within a community.

The diagram shows the different stages involved in a modern water plant producing water for domestic and industrial use.

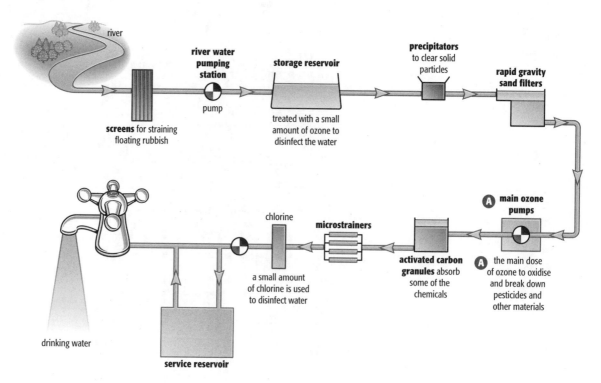

a What devices are used in the early stages of processing to remove insoluble debris and material? Include comments on the size of the material removed by these methods.

....

....

....

b What is the common purpose of treating the water with chlorine and/or ozone?

....

c What other purpose does treatment with ozone achieve?

....

d What type of chemical agent is ozone (O_3) behaving as in the reactions involved in part **c**?

....

e Countries that have insufficient rainfall, or where water supply is in great demand, may need to use other methods of producing clean water. In these countries, processes for **desalination** are used.

  i What does the term **desalination** mean?

  ....

  ii Name **two** methods that such countries use for desalination.

  ....

  iii Give **one** disadvantage of these methods of desalination.

  ....

f Tap water produced by a water treatment plant such as shown in the diagram is clean, but it is not pure. It will contain metal and non-metal ions dissolved from the rocks that the rivers and streams have flowed over.

  i Chloride ions are present in tap water. Describe a chemical test that would show the presence of chloride ions (Cl^-) in the water. Describe the test and what would be observed.

  ....

  ....

  ....

  ii One of the chlorides often present in tap water is sodium chloride. Give the word and balanced symbol equation for the reaction taking place in the test you have described above.

  sodium chloride + ... → .... + ...

  ....

  $NaCl$ + ... → .... + ...

  iii Give the ionic equation for the reaction taking place (include state symbols).

  ....

71

DEFINITIONS TO LEARN

limestone: a mineral form of calcium carbonate, $CaCO_3$ (other forms are chalk and marble)

lime: calcium oxide, CaO, – made from heating limestone in a lime kiln

limewater: a solution of calcium hydroxide, $Ca(OH)_2$ (aq), used as the analytical test for carbon dioxide

thermal decomposition: the breakdown of a compound into simpler substances by the action of heat

USEFUL REACTIONS AND THEIR EQUATIONS

calcium carbonate → calcium oxide + carbon dioxide

$CaCO_3(s) \rightarrow CaO(s) + CO_2(g)$

carbon dioxide + calcium hydroxide → calcium carbonate + water

$CO_2(g) + Ca(OH)_2 \rightarrow CaCO_3(s) + H_2O(l)$

Exercise C11.1 The action of heat on metal carbonates

This exercise will help you recall one of the major types of chemical reaction and help develop your skill at deducing conclusions from practical work.

The carbonates of many metallic elements decompose when heated.

a What type of reaction is this?

....

b Name the gas produced during the breakdown of a metal carbonate and describe a chemical test for this gas.

....

....

c A student investigates the breakdown of five different metal carbonates using the apparatus shown.

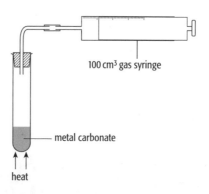

100 cm³ gas syringe

metal carbonate

heat

She heats a 0.010 mol sample of each carbonate using the blue flame of the same Bunsen burner. She measures the time it takes for 100 cm³ of gas to be collected in the gas syringe. The following table shows her results.

Carbonate	Time taken to collect 100 cm³ of gas / s
metal A carbonate	20
metal B carbonate	105
metal C carbonate	320
metal D carbonate	no gas produced after 1000
metal E carbonate	60

In fact, the student used samples of calcium carbonate, copper(II) carbonate, magnesium carbonate, sodium carbonate and zinc carbonate.

Given the information that the more reactive a metal is, the less easy it is to break down the metal carbonate, complete the table to show the identity of each metal: **A, B, C, D** and **E**.

Metal	Name of metal
A	....
B	....
C	....
D	....
E	....

d Write the chemical equation for the breakdown of zinc carbonate.

....

Exercise C11.2 Concrete chemistry

The use of limestone in cement is not a syllabus requirement, but this exercise will help your familiarity with questions asked in an unusual context.

Limestone is an important mineral resource. One use is in the making of cement. Cement is made by heating clay with crushed limestone. During this process, the calcium carbonate is first converted to calcium oxide (lime).

$$CaCO_3 \rightarrow CaO + CO_2$$

a What name is given to this type of chemical reaction?

....

Concrete is then made from cement, sand and water. When it has set, concrete is slightly porous. Rainwater can soak into concrete and some of the unreacted calcium oxide present dissolves to form calcium hydroxide.

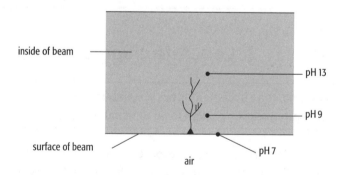

b Write an equation for this reaction that produces calcium hydroxide.

....

The aqueous calcium hydroxide in wet concrete is able to react with carbon dioxide in the air.

$$Ca(OH)_2 + CO_2 \rightarrow CaCO_3 + H_2O$$

The diagram shows how the pH can vary at different points inside a cracked concrete beam.

inside of beam

pH 13

pH 9

surface of beam

pH 7

air

c Describe the change in pH from the surface to the centre of the beam, and explain why this variation occurs.

....

....

....

....

d Research and describe briefly two other industrial uses for limestone in addition to making cement.

....

....

....

....

C12:
Organic chemistry

DEFINITIONS TO LEARN

hydrocarbon: a compound that contains carbon and hydrogen only

saturated hydrocarbon: a hydrocarbon that contains only single covalent bonds between the carbon atoms

alkane: a saturated hydrocarbon that contains only single covalent bonds between the carbon atoms of the chain; the simplest alkane is methane, CH_4

alkene: an unsaturated hydrocarbon that contains at least one double bond between two of the carbon atoms in the chain; the simplest alkene is ethene, C_2H_4

homologous series: a family of organic compounds with similar chemical properties as they contain the same functional group; for example, alkenes or alcohols

isomers: molecules with the same molecular formula but different structural formulae

substitution reaction: a reaction in which one or more hydrogen atoms in a hydrocarbon are replaced by atoms of another element

addition reaction: a reaction in which atoms, or groups, are added across a carbon–carbon double bond in an unsaturated molecule such as an alkene

fossil fuel: a fuel formed underground from previously living material by the action of heat and pressure over geological periods of time

cracking: a thermal decomposition reaction in which a long-chain saturated alkane is broken down to a shorter alkane, usually with the formation of an alkene

catalytic cracking: cracking carried out in the presence of a catalyst

monomer: the small molecules from which polymers are built by joining them together

polymer: a long-chain molecule made by joining many monomer molecules together

polymerisation: the process by which a long-chain polymer is made from its monomers

addition polymerisation: a polymerisation process in which the monomers contain a carbon–carbon double bond and polymerisation takes place by addition reactions

USEFUL REACTIONS AND THEIR EQUATIONS

methane + oxygen → carbon dioxide + water

$CH_4 + 2O_2 \rightarrow CO_2 + 2H_2O$ burning methane

ethanol + oxygen → carbon dioxide + water

$C_2H_5OH + 3O_2 \rightarrow 2CO_2 + 3H_2O$ burning ethanol

glucose → ethanol + carbon dioxide

$C_6H_{12}O_6 \rightarrow 2C_2H_5OH + 2CO_2$ fermentation

methane + chlorine → chloromethane + hydrogen chloride

$CH_4 + Cl_2 \rightarrow CH_3Cl + HCl$ substitution

decane → octane + ethene

$C_{10}H_{22} \rightarrow C_8H_{18} + C_2H_4$ cracking

$nC_2H_4 \rightarrow -(C_2H_4)_n-$

$nCH_2CHCl \rightarrow -(CH_2CHCl)_n-$ }   addition polymerisation

Exercise 12.1 Families of hydrocarbons

This exercise helps you revise the key features of the families of hydrocarbons and develops your understanding of the structures of organic compounds.

a Complete the passage using only words from the list.

bromine   alkanes   hydrogen   double   chlorine   chains   petroleum

methane   ethene   ethane   colourless   propane   alkenes

The chief source of organic compounds is the naturally occurring mixture of hydrocarbons known as

.... Hydrocarbons are compounds that contain carbon and ....

only. There are many hydrocarbons because of the ability of carbon atoms to join together to form long

.... There is a series of hydrocarbons with just single covalent bonds between the carbon

atoms in the molecule. These are saturated hydrocarbons, and they are called ....

The simplest of these saturated hydrocarbons has the formula CH_4 and is called ....

Unsaturated hydrocarbons can also occur. These molecules contain at least one carbon–carbon

.... bond. These compounds belong to the ...., a second

series of hydrocarbons. The simplest of this 'family' of unsaturated hydrocarbons has the formula C_2H_4

and is known as...................................... .

The test for an unsaturated hydrocarbon is to add the sample to..................................... water. It changes

colour from orange-brown to......................................if the hydrocarbon is unsaturated.

b The table shows the names, formulae and boiling points of the first members of the homologous series of unsaturated hydrocarbons. Complete the table by filling in the spaces.

Name	Formula	Boiling point / °C
....	C_2H_4	−102
propene	C_3H_6	−48
butene	C_4H_8	−7
pentene	C_5H_{10}	30
hexene	....	....

c Deduce the molecular formula of the alkene which has a relative molecular mass of 168.

....

Exercise 12.2 Unsaturated hydrocarbons (the alkenes)

This exercise develops your understanding of unsaturated hydrocarbons using an unfamiliar example.

Limonene is a colourless unsaturated hydrocarbon found in oranges and lemons. The structure of limonene is shown here.

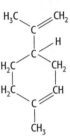

a On the structure, draw a circle around the bonds which make limonene an unsaturated hydrocarbon.

b What is the molecular formula of limonene?

....

c Describe the colour change which occurs when excess limonene is added to a few drops of bromine water.

....

The diagram shows how limonene can be extracted from lemon peel by steam distillation.

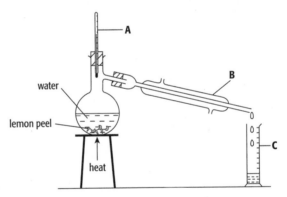

d State the name of the pieces of apparatus labelled **A**, **B** and **C**.

A... B... C...

When limonene undergoes incomplete combustion, carbon monoxide is formed.

e What do you understand by the term **incomplete combustion**?

....

....

f   State an adverse effect of carbon monoxide on health.

....

....

g   The structures of some compounds found in plants are shown below.

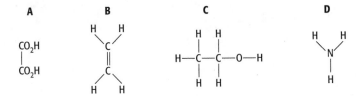

i   Which one of these compounds is produced by the fermentation of glucose? ....

ii   Which one of these compounds is a hydrocarbon? ....

h   All hydrocarbons are covalently bonded whether saturated or unsaturated. Draw 'dot-and-cross' diagrams for methane and ethane illustrating the arrangement of the bonding electrons. You only need to draw the outer electrons of the carbon atoms.

Exercise 12.3 The alcohols as fuels

The following exercise uses information relating to the alcohols to develop your understanding of these compounds and to enhance your presentation, analysis and interpretation of experimental data concerning their property as fuels.

The table shows the formulae of the first three members of the alcohol homologous series.

Alcohol	Formula
methanol	CH_3OH
ethanol	C_2H_5OH
propanol	C_3H_7OH

a   Use the information given to deduce the general formula for the alcohol homologous series.

....

Ethanol, the most significant of the alcohols, can be manufactured from either ethene or glucose.

b   Write an equation for the industrial production of ethanol from ethene and state the conditions under which the reaction takes place.

....

....

The fermentation (anaerobic respiration) of glucose by yeast can be represented by the following equation. The reaction is catalysed by the enzyme zymase. After a few days, the reaction stops. It has produced a 12% aqueous solution of ethanol.

$$C_6H_{12}O_6 \rightarrow 2C_2H_5OH + 2CO_2$$

c   Sketch a labelled diagram to show how fermentation can be carried out.

d   Suggest a reason why the reaction stops after a few days.

....

....

e Why is it essential that there is no oxygen in the reaction vessel?

....

....

f Name the products of the complete combustion of ethanol.

....

g Explain why ethanol made from ethene is a non-renewable fuel, but that made from glucose is a renewable fuel.

....

....

....

A student used this apparatus to investigate the amount of heat produced when ethanol was burnt.

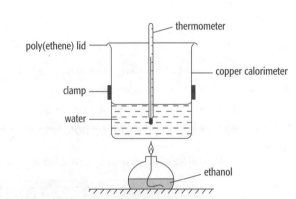

h Draw the structure of ethanol showing all atoms and bonds.

i Complete the equation for the complete combustion of ethanol.

$C_2H_5OH + 3O_2 \rightarrow$ .... $CO_2 +$ .... H_2O

j When 2.3 g of ethanol are burnt, 2.7 g of water are formed. Calculate the mass of water formed when 13.8 g of ethanol are burnt.

....

....

....

The experiment was later adapted to compare the heat released by burning four different alcohols. Each burner in turn was weighed and then the alcohol was allowed to burn until the temperature of the water had risen by 5 °C. The flame was then extinguished and the burner re-weighed. The results obtained are shown on the following page.

Alcohol	Formula	Mass of alcohol burnt / g
methanol	CH_3OH	0.90
ethanol	C_2H_5OH	0.70
propan-1-ol	C_3H_7OH	0.62
pentan-1-ol	$C_5H_{11}OH$	0.57

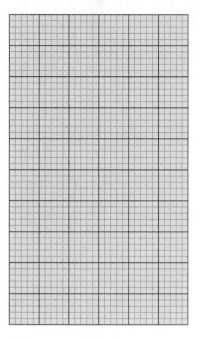

k Plot a graph showing how the mass of alcohol required varies with the number of carbon atoms in the alcohol used. Draw a smooth curve through the points.

Use the checklist below to give yourself a mark for your graph. For each point, award yourself:
- **2 marks if you did it really well**
- **1 mark if you made a good attempt at it, and partly succeeded**
- **0 marks if you did not try to do it, or did not succeed.**

Self-assessment checklist for graphs:

Check point	Marks awarded	
	You	**Your teacher**
You have drawn the axes with a ruler, using most of the width and height of the grid.		
You have used a good scale for the *x*-axis and the *y*-axis, going up in useful proportions.		
You have labelled the axes correctly, giving the correct units for the scales on both axes.		
You have plotted each point precisely and correctly.		
You have used a small, neat cross or dot for each point.		
You have drawn a single, clear best-fit line through the points.		
You have ignored any anomalous results when drawing the line.		
Total (out of 14)		

12–14 Excellent.

10–11 Good.

7–9 A good start, but you need to improve quite a bit.

5–6 Poor. Try this same graph again, using a new sheet of graph paper.

1–4 Very poor. Read through all the criteria again, and then try the same graph again.

l Predict the mass of butanol, C_4H_9OH, which, on combustion, would raise the temperature of the water by 15 °C.

....

m Suggest a reason why the same temperature rise (15 °C) was used in each experiment.

....

....

Exercise C12.4 Essential processes of the petrochemical industry

> **This exercise aids you in recalling and understanding two of the main processes of the petrochemical industry.**

Petroleum (crude oil) is a raw material which is processed in an oil refinery. Two of the processes used are **fractional distillation** and **cracking**.

a The diagram shows the fractional distillation of petroleum. Give the name and a major use for each fraction.

A: ....

B: ....

C: ....

D: ....

E: ....

A: ....

B: ....

C: ....

D: ....

E: ....

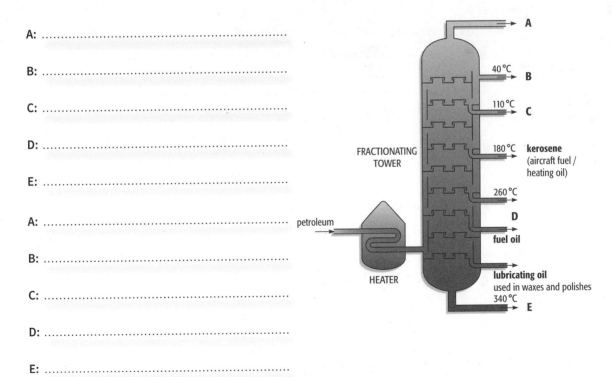

The table below shows the percentage by mass of some of these different fractions in petroleum. Also shown is the demand for each fraction expressed as a percentage.

Fraction	Number of carbon atoms per molecule	Percentage in petroleum / %	Percentage needed by the oil refinery to supply demand / %
A	1–4	4	11
B	5–9	11	22
C	10–14	12	20
kerosine	14–20	18	15
waxes and E	over 20	23	4

b Which physical property is used to separate petroleum by fractional distillation?

....

c Define the term **cracking**.

....

....

d Use information from the table to explain how cracking helps an oil refinery match the supply of gasoline (petrol) with the demand for gasoline.

....

....

....

e The hydrocarbon $C_{15}H_{32}$ can be cracked to make propene and one other hydrocarbon.

   i   Write an equation for this reaction.

....

   ii   Draw the structure of propene.

Exercise C12.5 Addition polymerisation

> This exercise will help you practise the representation of polymers and develop your understanding of their uses and the issues involved.

a   Poly(ethene) is a major plastic used for making a wide variety of containers. Complete these sentences about poly(ethene) using words from this list.

acids	addition	condensation	ethane
polymerisation	ethene	monomers	polymer

Poly(ethene) is a .... formed by the .... of

.... molecules. In this reaction, the starting molecules can be described as

....; the process is known as ....

b   Draw the structure of poly(ethene) showing **at least two** repeat units.

DEFINITIONS TO LEARN

titration: a method of finding the amount of a substance in a solution

precipitation: the sudden appearance of a solid produced in a chemical reaction

ionic equation: an equation showing only those ions that participate in a reaction and the product of that reaction

USEFUL REACTIONS AND THEIR EQUATIONS

$AgNO_3(aq) + NaCl(aq) \rightarrow AgCl(s) + NaNO_3(aq)$	or	$Ag^+(aq) + Cl^-(aq) \rightarrow AgCl(s)$
$Ba(NO_3)_2(aq) + CuSO_4(aq) \rightarrow BaSO_4(s) + Cu(NO_3)_2(aq)$	or	$Ba^{2+}(aq) + SO_4^{2-}(aq) \rightarrow BaSO_4(s)$
$FeSO_4(aq) + 2NaOH(aq) \rightarrow Fe(OH)_2(s) + Na_2SO_4(aq)$	or	$Fe^{2+}(aq) + 2OH^-(aq) \rightarrow Fe(OH)_2(s)$

Exercise C13.1 Titration analysis

> This exercise will help you remember some of the basic procedures involved in practical work, including points that will be checked on as you carry out practical work safely and rigorously.

a Choose words from the list below to complete the passage.

accurate	catalyst	thymolphthalein	indicator	measuring cylinder
pipette	qualitative	neutralised	quantitative	three

There are situations when chemists need to know how much of a substance is present or how concentrated a solution of a substance is. This type of experiment is part of what is known as .... analysis. One experimental method used here is titration.

The important pieces of apparatus used in titration are a burette and a .... When an acid is titrated against an alkali, methyl orange can be used as the .... so that we know that the acid has just .... the alkali. A few drops of .... can be used as an alternative to methyl orange. The experiment is repeated several times, often until .... results have been obtained that are in close agreement with each other.

b As part of an experiment to determine the value of x in the formula for iron(II) sulfate crystals (FeSO$_4$.xH$_2$O), a student titrated a solution of these crystals with 0.0200 mol/dm³ potassium manganate(VII) (solution **A**).

A 25.0 cm³ sample of the iron(II) sulfate solution was measured into a conical titration flask. Solution **A** was run from a burette into the flask until an end-point was reached. Four titrations were carried out. The diagrams show parts of the burette before and after each titration.

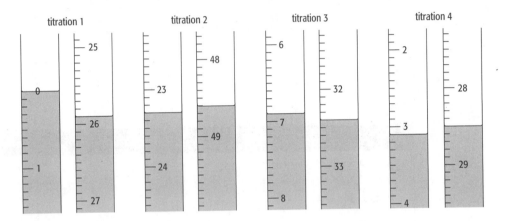

i Use the diagrams to complete the table of results.

Titration number	1	2	3	4
Final burette reading / cm³	....	....	....	....
First burette reading / cm³	....	....	....	....
Volume of solution A / cm³	....	....	....	....
Best titration results (✓)				

Tick (✓) the columns with the best titration results.

Using these results, the average volume of **A** was .... cm³.

ii Solution **A** is 0.0200 mol/dm³ potassium manganate(VII). Calculate how many moles of KMnO$_4$ were present in the titrated volume of **A** calculated in part **i**.

iii What type of reaction takes place between the iron(II) sulfate solution and solution **A**?

....

iv Potassium manganate(VII) is purple. What was the colour change at the end-point?

Change from .... to ....

87

Exercise C13.2 Chemical analysis

This exercise will help familiarise you with some of the analytical tests and the strategy behind them. Remember that these tests might come up on the written papers as well as on the practical papers.

a The following table shows the tests that some students did on substance **A** and the conclusions they made from their observations.

i Complete the table by describing these observations and suggest the test and observation which led to the conclusion in test **4**.

Test	Observation	Conclusion
1 Solid **A** was dissolved in water and the solution divided into three parts for tests **2**, **3** and **4**.	....	**A** does not contain a transition metal.
2 i To the first part, aqueous sodium hydroxide was added until a change was seen.	....	**A** may contain Zn^{2+} ions or Al^{3+} ions.
ii Excess aqueous sodium hydroxide was added to the mixture from **i**.	....	
3 i To the second part aqueous ammonia was added until a change was seen.	....	The presence of Zn^{2+} ions is confirmed in **A**.
ii An excess of aqueous ammonia was added to the mixture from **i**.	....	
4	....	**A** contains I^- ions.

ii Give the name and formula of compound **A**.

....

b A mixture of powdered crystals contains both ammonium ions (NH_4^+) and zinc ions (Zn^{2+}). The two salts contain the same anion (negative ion).

The table below shows the results of tests carried out by a student.

i Complete the table of observations made by the student.

Test	Observations
1 A sample of the solid mixture was dissolved in distilled water. The solution was acidified with dilute HCl(aq) and a solution of Ba(NO$_3$)$_2$ added.	A white precipitate was formed.
2 A sample of the solid was placed in a test tube. NaOH(aq) was added and the mixture warmed. A piece of moist red litmus paper was held at the mouth of the tube.	The solid dissolved and pungent fumes were given off. The litmus paper turned ...., indicating the presence of .... ions.
3 A sample of the solid was dissolved in distilled water to give a ....solution. NaOH(aq) was added dropwise until in excess.	A .... precipitate was formed which was .... in excess alkali.
4 A further sample of the solid was dissolved in distilled water. Concentrated ammonia solution (NH$_3$(aq)) was added dropwise until in excess.	A .... precipitate was formed. On addition of excess alkali, the precipitate was ....

ii Give the names and formulae of the two salts in the mixture.

....

iii Give the name and formula of the precipitate formed in tests **3** and **4**.

....

c   A mixture of two solids, **P** and **Q**, was analysed.

Solid **P** was the water-soluble salt aluminium sulfate, $Al_2(SO_4)_3$, and solid **Q** was an insoluble salt.

The tests on the mixture and some of the observations are reported in the following table.

i   Complete the observations in the table.

Tests	Observations
Distilled water was added to the mixture of **P** and **Q** in a boiling tube. The boiling tube was shaken and the contents of the tube then filtered, keeping the filtrate and residue for the following tests. The filtrate was divided into five test tubes in order to carry out tests **1** to **5**.	
Tests on the filtrate 1 Appearance of the first sample of the filtrate.	....
2 Drops of aqueous sodium hydroxide were added to the second portion of the solution and the test tube shaken. Excess aqueous sodium hydroxide was then added to the test tube.	....
3 Aqueous ammonia was added to the third portion, dropwise and then in excess.	....

Tests	Observations
4 Dilute nitric acid was added to the fourth portion of the solution followed by aqueous silver nitrate.	....
5 Dilute nitric acid was added to the fifth portion of the solution and then aqueous barium nitrate.	....
Tests on the residue Dilute hydrochloric acid was added to the residue. The gas given off was tested. Excess aqueous sodium hydroxide was added to the mixture in the test tube.	rapid effervescence observed limewater turned milky white precipitate, insoluble in excess

ii Name the gas given off in the tests on the residue.

....

iii What conclusions can you draw about solid **Q** from the observations made? Explain your reasoning.

....

....

....

Exercise C13.3 Planning a controlled experiment

The questions in this exercise illustrate the issues faced when designing experiments that will give you results that are clear. They will help you think through which conditions need to be controlled in a given situation so that a fair test can be carried out. They do not show all possible situations but will give an idea of the range of investigations you may encounter.

a Sudso is a washing powder which has been designed to work best at 30 °C. Mr Jones has always done his washing at 50 °C and thinks that 50 °C will work better.

Devise an experiment to discover which temperature is best for the washing powder Sudso.

....

....

....

....

....

....

....

....

b Harjit buys some cheap saffron from a street trader in Delhi. His wife thinks it is too brightly coloured and must be fake. She has some genuine saffron which is paler in colour.

Devise an experiment to compare the two samples of saffron to see if an artificial colour has been added to the saffron that Harjit bought.

....

....

....

....

....

....

....

c Urea, $(NH_2)_2CO$, is an organic compound which is soluble in both water and an organic solvent such as ethanol.

Urea has an important place in the history of chemistry. The discovery by Friedrich Wöhler in 1828 that urea can be produced and crystallised from inorganic starting materials showed for the first time that a substance previously known only as a by-product of life could be made in the laboratory without any biological starting materials. This finding contradicted the view, known as **vitalism** and widely held at the time, that the chemistry of life was totally different from the inorganic world.

A computer model of the urea molecule

i Devise an experiment to find which solvent, water or ethanol, is better at dissolving urea. Comment clearly on the conditions that must be kept constant.

....

....

....

....

....

....

....

ii You have found an old bottle of powdered urea in the lab. Describe, using either solvent, how you could prepare some good crystals of urea from the powder.

....

....

....

....

d Antibac and Cleano are two products used for cleaning kitchen surfaces. One contains a chlorine bleach as the cleaning agent, while the other contains about 60% ethanol.

i Describe a test that would show which product contains the bleach.

....

ii Describe a way of finding out how much ethanol the other product contains.

....

....

....

....

Exercise C13.4 Chemical testing and evaluation

> This exercise links various chemical tests with the skills of designing experiments so that they give clear answers to the questions raised about a particular sample. The exercise will familiarise you with some of the analytical tests and experimental methods. At the end of the exercise, there is a checklist on which you can assess how well you have understood the key features of this type of practical planning.

a   Limestone and chalk are impure forms of calcium carbonate. Calcium carbonate reacts with hydrochloric acid to form calcium chloride, carbon dioxide and water.

You are provided with lumps of limestone and chalk and hydrochloric acid together with a full range of lab apparatus. Devise an experiment to discover which of these two types of rock contains the higher percentage of calcium carbonate.

....

....

....

....

....

....

....

....

b   The label on a 500 ml bottle of **Harcourt Spring Water** states the following:

Composition mg/litre
calcium 55 mg
magnesium 16 mg
potassium 2 mg
sodium 15 mg
hydrogencarbonate 240 mg
sulfate 28 mg
nitrate 6 mg
chloride 11 mg

Harcourt Spring Water

Dry residue after evaporation
255 mg
pH 4.6

i   What are the formulae of the following ions?

Potassium ion: ....

Magnesium ion: ....

Nitrate ion: ....

Hydrogencarbonate ion: ....

ii Describe a test to confirm the presence of sodium ions in the water.

....

iii How could you confirm that the pH of the water was 4.6?

....

iv Describe how you could confirm the amount of dry residue given on the label.

....

....

....

....

....

c The metals magnesium, iron and zinc all react exothermically with hydrochloric acid to form chloride salts. For example:

Zn + 2HCl → **ZnC**l_2 + H$_2$

i How could you test a salt solution to show that it contained zinc ions?

....

....

....

ii Describe an experiment, using the reaction of the metals with acid, which would place the three metals (magnesium, iron and zinc) in order of reactivity.

....

....

....

....

....

d You are provided with magnesium ribbon and sulfuric acid together with normal laboratory apparatus.

Describe an experiment to show the effect of concentration on the rate of a chemical reaction.

....

....

....

....

....

....

....

Use the checklist below to give yourself a mark for your experiment planning.

For each point, award yourself:

- **2 marks if you did it really well**
- **1 mark if you made a good attempt at it, and partly succeeded**
- **0 mark if you did not try to do it, or did not succeed.**

Self-assessment checklist for planning experiments:

Check point	Marks awarded	
	You	Your teacher
You have stated the variable to be changed (independent variable)		
You have stated the range of this variable you will use, and how you will vary it.		
You have stated at least three important variables to be kept constant (and not included ones that are not important).		
You have stated the variable to be measured (dependent variable), how you will measure it and when you will measure it.		
You have drawn up an outline results chart where appropriate.		
If a hypothesis is being tested, you have predicted what the results will be if the hypothesis is correct.		
Total (out of 12)		

10–12   Excellent.

8–9   Good.

5–7   A good start, but you need to improve quite a bit.

3–4   Poor. Try this same plan again.

1–2   Very poor. Read through all the criteria again, and then try the same plan again.

Exercise C13.5 Experimental design

This exercise emphasises the considerations that are important when planning and evaluating an experimental method.

How is the rate of a reaction affected by temperature?

The reaction between dilute hydrochloric acid and sodium thiosulfate solution produces a fine yellow precipitate that clouds the solution. This means that the rate of this reaction can be found by measuring the time taken for a cross (×) under the reaction to become hidden.

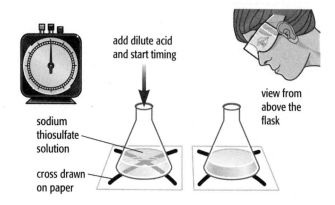

add dilute acid and start timing

view from above the flask

sodium thiosulfate solution

cross drawn on paper

a You are asked to design an experiment to see how changing the temperature of the solutions mixed affects the rate of the reaction.

You are provided with the following apparatus and solutions:

- several 100 cm^3 conical flasks of the same size and shape
- dilute hydrochloric acid solution (0.5 moles per dm^3)
- sodium thiosulfate solution – a colourless solution (0.5 moles per dm^3)
- several 50 cm^3 measuring cylinders
- a piece of white card and a felt-tip marker pen
- a stopclock
- a water bath that is thermostatically controlled so that the temperature can be adjusted – flasks of solution can be placed in this to adjust to the required temperature
- two thermometers
- and any other normal lab apparatus.

Your description should include:

- a statement of the aim of the experiment – comment on which factors in the experiment need to be kept constant and why
- a description of the method for carrying out the experiment – this should be a list of instructions to another student
- safety – put in a comment on what **safety precautions** you need to take and why.

....

....

....

....

....

....

....

b Below are the results of tests carried out at five different temperatures. In each case, 50 cm³ of aqueous sodium thiosulfate was poured into a flask. 10 cm³ of hydrochloric acid was added to the flask. The initial and final temperatures were measured.

Use the thermometer diagrams to record all of the initial and final temperatures in the table.

i Complete the table of results to show the average temperatures.

Experiment	Thermometer diagram at start	Initial temperature /°C	Thermometer diagram at end	Final temperature /°C	Average temperature /°C	Time for cross to disappear / s
1		....		....	....	130
2		....		....	....	79
3		....		....	....	55
4		....		....	....	33
5		....		....	....	26

ii Plot a graph of the time taken for the cross to disappear versus the average temperature on the grid, and draw a smooth line graph.

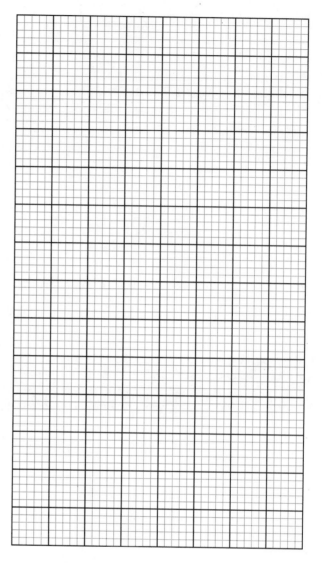

c In which experiment was the speed of reaction greatest? ....

d Explain why the speed was greatest in this experiment.

....

....

e Why were the same volume of sodium thiosulfate solution and the same volume of hydrochloric acid used in each experiment? Why do the conical flasks used in each test run need to be of the same dimensions?

....

....

f From the graph, deduce the time for the cross to disappear if the experiment was to be repeated at 70 °C. Show clearly on the grid how you worked out your answer.

....

g Sketch on the grid the curve you would expect if all the experiments were repeated using 50 cm³ of more concentrated sodium thiosulfate solution.

h How would it be possible to achieve a temperature of around 0 to 5 °C?

....

i Explain **one** change that could be made to the experimental method to obtain more accurate results.

....

....

Use the checklist below to give yourself a mark for your graph. For each point, award yourself:
- **2 marks if you did it really well**
- **1 mark if you made a good attempt at it, and partly succeeded**
- **0 marks if you did not try to do it, or did not succeed.**

Self-assessment checklist for graphs:

Check point	Marks awarded	
	You	Your teacher
You have drawn the axes with a ruler, using most of the width and height of the grid.		
You have used a good scale for the *x*-axis and the *y*-axis, going up in useful proportions.		
You have labelled the axes correctly, giving the correct units for the scales on both axes.		
You have plotted each point precisely and correctly.		
You have used a small, neat dot or cross for each point.		
You have drawn a single, clear best-fit line through the points – using a ruler for a straight line.		
You have ignored any anomalous results when drawing the line.		
Total (out of 14)		

12–14 Excellent.

10–11 Good.

7–9 A good start, but you need to improve quite a bit.

5–6 Poor. Try this same graph again, using a new sheet of graph paper.

1–4 Very poor. Read through all the criteria again, and then try the same graph again.

Exercise C1.1
Changing physical state

a A = solid;   B = solid and liquid (melting is in process);
    C = liquid;   D = liquid and gas (boiling is taking place)

b 17 °C

c 115 °C

d The temperature remains constant until the change of state is complete.

e The melting point and boiling point are not those of water.

f The kinetic model states that the **particles** in a liquid and a **gas** are in constant motion. In a gas, the particles are far apart from each other and their motion is said to be **random**. The particles in a solid are held in fixed positions in a regular **lattice**. In a solid, the particles can only **vibrate** about their fixed positions.

Liquids and gases are fluid states. When particles move in a fluid they can collide with each other. When they collide, they bounce off each other in **different** directions. If two gases or liquids are mixed the different types of particle **spread** out and get mixed up. This process is called **diffusion**.

At the same **temperature** particles that have a lower mass move faster than those with higher mass. This means that the lighter particles will spread and mix more quickly; the lighter particles are said to **diffuse** faster than the heavier particles.

g **i** radon

    ii radon and nitrogen

    iii nitrogen

    iv cobalt

    v The sample of ethanoic acid is impure – the presence of impurities raises the boiling point of a substance.

Exercise C1.2
Plotting a cooling curve

a

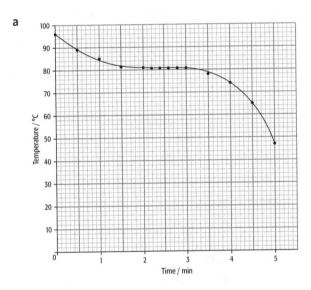

b The substance is freezing (solidifying); turning from liquid to solid.

c The temperature stays constant because energy is being released as the substance solidifies; the molecules are giving out heat as they stop moving from place to place and become organised in a structured lattice arrangement; in the solid the molecules can only vibrate about fixed points; the heat released keeps the temperature constant until all the substance is solid.

d You would need to use an oil bath (in place of the water bath) so that the higher temperature could be reached.

e i

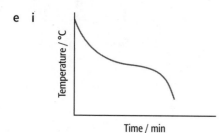

ii The curve flattens but the temperature does not stay constant while the wax solidifies. This is because wax is a mixture of substances, not a pure compound.

f i Water ice has a film of liquid water on its surface; solid carbon dioxide is dry (no liquid film).

ii The carbon dioxide is under pressure in the fire extinguisher.

iii Hoar frost is a powdery **white** frost caused when solid **ice** forms from **humid** air. The solid surface on which it is formed must be **colder** than the **surrounding** air. Water vapour is deposited on a surface as fine ice **crystals** without going through the **liquid** phase.

Exercise C2.1
Diffusion, solubility and separation

a i The purple crystals are soluble in water so the water begins to break up the crystals, and particles (ions) from the solid move into the water. This continues until all the solid dissolves. The particles then move through the liquid and spread out through the liquid until the solution is evenly coloured throughout.

ii a shorter time – if the temperature was higher, the particles would be moving faster as they would have more energy / the process of diffusion would take place more quickly

b i The analysis would be done by paper chromatography. A piece of filter paper (chromatography paper) would be set up with a pencil line drawn across the bottom, samples of the green solution would be spotted on the line and the bottom edge of the paper then dipped carefully in a solvent (ethanol, for example). The solvent would rise up the paper and different substances would move at different rates up the paper. One spot would be chlorophyll (green), but other (yellow) spots would be seen.

ii

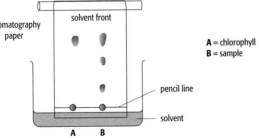

chromatography paper

solvent front

pencil line

solvent

A   B

A = chlorophyll
B = sample

c

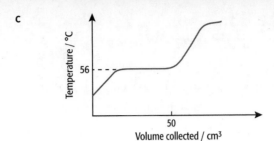

Exercise C2.2
Chromatography at the races

a Two factors:

- the length of time the chromatogram is run (developed) for
- the solubility of the substance in the solvent – the more soluble the substance, the further it runs

b Horse **C**; paracetamol

c It is used as a painkiller.

d $R_f = \dfrac{\text{distance travelled by the substance}}{\text{distance travelled by the solvent}} = \dfrac{7.5}{10} = 0.75$

Note that you have a partial check on your answer here as the R_f value must be less than 1.

Exercise C3.1
Atomic structure

a Atoms are made up of three different particles: **protons** which are positively charged; **neutrons** which have no charge; and **electrons** which are negatively charged. The negatively charged particles are arranged in different **energy levels** (shells) around the **nucleus** of the atom. The particles with a negligible mass are the **electrons**. All atoms of the same element contain the same number of **protons** and **electrons**. Atoms of the same element with different numbers of **neutrons** are known as **isotopes**.

b The electrons in an atom are arranged in a series of **shells** around the nucleus. These shells are also called **energy** levels. In an atom, the shell **nearest** to the nucleus fills first, then the next shell, and so on. There is room for

- up to **two** electrons in the first shell
- up to **eight** electrons in the second shell
- up to **eight** electrons in the third shell.

(There are 18 electrons in total when the three shells are completely full.)

The elements in the Periodic Table are organised in the same way as the electrons fill the shells. Shells fill from **left** to **right** across the **rows** of the Periodic Table.

- The first shell fills up first from **hydrogen** to helium.
- The second shell fills next from lithium to **neon**.
- Eight **electrons** go into the third shell from sodium to argon.
- Then the fourth shell starts to fill from potassium.

Exercise C3.2
The first four periods

a lithium and sodium (Li, Na)

b chromium and copper (Cr, Cu)

c helium (He)

d bromine (Br)

e carbon (C)

f sulfur (S)

g helium, neon and krypton (He, Ne, Kr)

h copper (Cu)

i calcium (Ca)

j magnesium (Mg)

Exercise C3.3
The chemical bonding in simple molecules

a

Name of compound	Formula	Drawing of structure	Molecular model
hydrogen chloride	*HCl*	H – C*l*	
water	H_2O	H^{O}H	
ammonia	NH_3	H–N–H, H	
methane	CH_4	H, H–C–H, H	
ethene	C_2H_4	H,H C=C H,H	
carbon dioxide	CO_2	0 = C = 0	

b   i   Graphite conducts electricity because not all of the outer electrons of the carbon atoms are used in the covalent bonding that holds the atoms together in the layers. These 'free' electrons are able to move in between the layers. They can be made to move in one direction when a voltage is applied.

ii   Graphite acts as a lubricant because there are only weak forces between the layers of carbon atoms in the structure. The layers can be made to move over each other if a force is applied.

Exercise C3.4
The nature of ionic lattices

Property	Explanation

Property

The solution of an ionic compound in water is a good conductor of electricity – such ionic substances are electrolytes.

Ionic crystals have a regular shape. All the crystals of each solid ionic compound are the same shape. Whatever the size of the crystal, the angles between the faces of the crystal are always the same.

Ionic compounds have relatively high melting points.

When an ionic compound is heated above its melting point, the molten compound is a good conductor of electricity.

Explanation

The ions in the giant ionic structure are always arranged in the same regular way – see the diagram.

The giant ionic structure is held together by the strong attraction between the positive and negative ions. It takes a lot of energy to break down the regular arrangement of ions.

In a molten ionic compound, the positive and negative ions can move around – they can move to the electrodes when a voltage is applied.

In a solution of an ionic compound, the positive metal ions and the negative non-metal ions can move around – they can move to the electrodes when a voltage is applied.

Exercise C4.1
Formulae of ionic compounds

a **i** CuO

   ii Na_2CO_3

   iii $ZnSO_4$

   iv $AgNO_3$

   v $MgBr_2$

   vi $(NH_4)_2SO_4$

   vii Mg_3N_2

   viii K_3PO_4

   ix $Fe(OH)_3$

   x $CrCl_3$

b **i** 1:1

   ii 1:2

   iii 3:2

   iv 1:3:3

   v 2:8:1:4

c **i** 2:1

   ii K_2O

d **i**

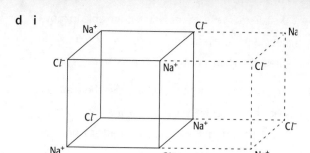

ii

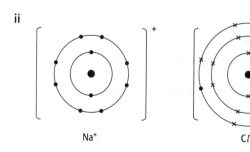

iii

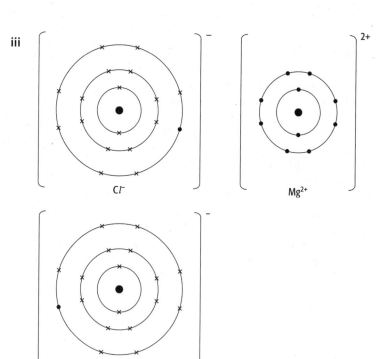

Exercise C4.2
Making magnesium oxide – a quantitative investigation

a The mass of magnesium oxide produced increases if more magnesium is used. The increase is linear (directly proportional).

b

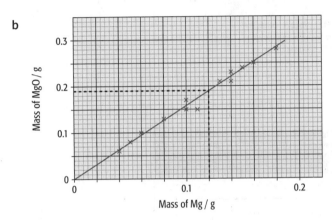

mass of MgO produced = 0.19 g

Note that your answer may differ slightly because your line of best fit may be slightly different. A sensible range of answers would be allowed in the exam.

c 0.19 − 0.12 = 0.07 g

d $\frac{0.07}{0.12} \cdot 24 = 14g$

e from the experiment:

	Mg	O
mass	24	14
number of moles	$\frac{24}{24} = 1.0$	$\frac{14}{16} = 0.88$
whole number ratio	1	1

The ratio of moles of Mg to moles of O is 1 : 1

so the formula is MgO.

Exercise C4.3
The analysis of titration results

Table of results

Burette readings / cm³	Experiment 1	Experiment 2
final reading	10.6	36.1
initial reading	0.0	14.9
difference	10.6	21.2

a neutralisation

b hydrochloric acid + sodium hydroxide
   → sodium chloride + water

c yellow → red

d Experiment 2

e More acid used in experiment **2** to neutralise the same volume of sodium hydroxide, so acid solution in this experiment must be a more dilute solution. Twice as much acid used, so this acid solution must be half the concentration of that used in experiment **1** (solution **P**).

f volume of solution **P** needed = 2.5 × 10.6 = 26.5 cm³
   explanation: using 25.0 cm³ of sodium hydroxide instead of 10 cm³ so will need $\frac{25}{10} = 2.5$ times the volume of acid to neutralise

g Use a pipette rather than a measuring cylinder to measure the volume of sodium hydroxide.

Exercise C4.4
Calculating formula masses

a

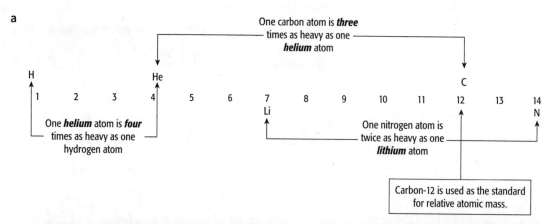

b

Molecule	Chemical formula	Number of atoms or ions involved	Relative formula mass
oxygen	O_2	2O	$2 \times 16 = 32$
carbon dioxide	CO_2	1C and 2O	$1 \times 12 + 2 \times 16 = \mathbf{44}$
water	H_2O	2H and 1O	$\mathbf{2 \times 1 + 16 = 18}$
ammonia	NH_3	1N and 3H	$\mathbf{14 + 3 \times 1 = 17}$
calcium carbonate	$CaCO_3$	$1Ca^{2+}$ and $1CO_3^{2-}$	$\mathbf{40 + 12 + 3 \times 16 = 100}$
magnesium oxide	MgO	$1Mg^{2+}$ and $1O^{2-}$	$1 \times 24 + 1 \times 16 = \mathbf{40}$
ammonium nitrate	NH_4NO_3	$1NH_4^+$ and $\mathbf{1NO_3^-}$	$2 \times 14 + \mathbf{4 \times 1} + 3 \times 16 = 80$
propanol	C_3H_7OH	3C, **8H** and 1O	$3 \times 12 + 8 \times 1 + \mathbf{1 \times 16} = 60$

Exercise C4.5
A sense of proportion in chemistry

a 5 tonnes zinc oxide $\rightarrow$ 4 tonnes zinc

so 20 tonnes zinc oxide $\rightarrow 4 \cdot \dfrac{20}{5} = \mathbf{16\ tonnes\ zinc}$

or $\dfrac{4}{5} = \dfrac{x}{20}$ so $x = 4 \cdot \dfrac{20}{5} = 16$ tonnes of zinc

b 17 tonnes of ammonia are produced from 14 tonnes nitrogen

so 34 tonnes of ammonia will be produced from $14 \cdot \dfrac{34}{17}$

$= \mathbf{28\ tonnes\ of\ nitrogen}$

or $\dfrac{14}{17} = \dfrac{x}{34}$ so $x = 14 \cdot \dfrac{34}{17} = 28$ tonnes of nitrogen

c 12 C atoms + 22 H atoms + 11 O atoms = 45 atoms

d $C_2H_4O_2$

Exercise C4.6
Finding the mass of 5 cm of magnesium ribbon

a

Experiment number	Volume of hydrogen collected / cm^3
1	85
2	79
3	82
average	**82**

The results are not equal because of the difficulty in cutting exactly equal lengths of magnesium ribbon. Also the pieces of ribbon may not be exactly the same thickness or width; or gas may be lost as the magnesium is allowed to fall into the flask; or there may have been air in the measuring cylinder before starting.

b from equation: 24 g of magnesium (1 mole) $\rightarrow$ 24 000 cm^3 of hydrogen so 1 cm^3 of hydrogen produced from $\frac{24}{24000} = 0.001$ g of magnesium and 82 cm^3 of hydrogen produced from $0.001 \times 82 = \mathbf{0.082\,g}$

c 24 g of magnesium $\rightarrow$ 120 g of magnesium sulfate so 0.082 g will give $\frac{120}{24} \times 0.082 = \mathbf{0.41\,g}$

The answers to **b** and **c** could be calculated by other proportionality methods.

d The key factor here is that 24 g of magnesium will produce 120 g of dried anhydrous magnesium sulfate (MgSO$_4$) (see the equation).

- Weigh out a known mass of magnesium ribbon.
- React it with excess dilute sulfuric acid until no more gas is given off and no magnesium remains.
- Transfer the solution to a beaker of known mass.
- Heat the solution to dryness, taking care to avoid spitting.

- Allow to cool and weigh the beaker and residue.
- Filter, dry and weigh the crystals carefully.
- From the data above, calculate the mass of crystals that 5 cm would have given.

Exercise C4.7
Reacting volumes of gases

a 75 cm^3

b 25 cm^3

c 50 cm^3

d $2NO \quad + \quad O_2 \quad \rightarrow \quad 2NO_2$

 50 cm^3 $\quad$ **25** cm^3 $\quad$ **50** cm^3

Exercise C5.1
The nature of electrolysis

Changes taking place during electrolysis

During electrolysis ionic compounds are decomposed by the passage of an electric current. For this to happen, the compound must be either *molten* or in *solution*. Electrolysis can occur when an electric *current* passes through a molten *electrolyte*. The two rods dipping into the electrolyte are called the *electrodes*. In this situation, metals are deposited at the *cathode* and non-metals are formed at the *anode*.

When the ionic compound is dissolved in water, the electrolysis can be more complex. Generally, during electrolysis *positive* ions move towards the *cathode* and negative ions move towards the *anode*. At the negative electrode (cathode) the metal or *hydrogen* ions gain electrons and form metal atoms or hydrogen *molecules*. At the positive electrode (anode) certain non-metal ions *lose* electrons and *oxygen* or chlorine is produced.

Examples of electrolysis in industry

There are several important industrial applications of electrolysis; the most important economically being the electrolysis of *molten* aluminium oxide to produce aluminium. The aluminium oxide is mixed with molten *cryolite* to *lower* the melting point of the electrolyte.

A *concentrated* aqueous solution of sodium chloride contains *sodium*, chloride, hydrogen and *hydroxide* ions. When this solution is electrolysed, *hydrogen* rather than sodium is discharged at the negative electrode. The solution remaining is sodium hydroxide.

When a solution of copper(II) sulfate is electrolysed using *copper* electrodes, an unusual thing happens and the copper atoms of the *positive* electrode (anode) go into solution as copper ions. At the cathode the copper ions turn into copper atoms, and the metal is deposited on this electrode. This can be used as a method of refining or *purifying* impure copper.

Exercise C5.2
Making and 'breaking' copper chloride

Synthesising copper(II) chloride

a   malleable and ductile

b   green

c   Chlorine gas is toxic (poisonous).

d   exothermic – there is a flame produced / the metal film flares as it reacts

   The fact that the metal is a thin sheet means that it has a large surface area to react with the chlorine gas.

e   The pale blue-green colour of the solution suggests that a copper(II) salt has been produced.

f $Cu + Cl_2 \rightarrow CuCl_2$

g   zinc chloride

Decomposing copper(II) chloride

a   copper(II) chloride $\rightarrow$ copper + chlorine

   $CuCl_2 \rightarrow Cu + Cl_2$

b   Electrolysis is the breakdown of an ionic compound, molten or in aqueous solution, by the passage of electricity.

c   A piece of damp (moist) litmus paper is held in the gas: it is bleached white.

d   i   It must be carried out in a fume cupboard.

   ii   Dip a piece of litmus paper in the solution around the positive electrode: it will be bleached because chlorine is soluble in water.

e   endothermic – electrical energy is used to split the compound into its elements

f   at the anode: $2Cl^-(aq) \rightarrow Cl_2(g) + 2e^-$

   at the cathode: $Cu^{2+}(aq) + 2e^- \rightarrow Cu(s)$

Exercise C6.1
Energy diagrams

a In an exothermic reaction, the ***reactants*** have more energy than the ***products***. This means that ΔH is ***negative***. The difference in energy is ***given out*** as heat.

The temperature of the surroundings ***increases*** / ~~decreases~~.

b In an endothermic reaction, the ***products*** have more energy than the ***reactants***. This means that ΔH is ***positive***. The difference in energy is ***taken in*** from the surroundings.

The temperature of the surroundings ~~increases~~ / ***decreases***.

Exercise C6.2
The collision theory of reaction rates

Factor affecting the reaction	Types of reaction affected	Change made in the condition	Effect on rate of reaction
concentration	all reactions involving solutions or reactions involving gases	an increase in the concentration of one, or both, of the ***reactants (reacting substances)*** means there are more particles in the same volume	increases the rate of reaction as the particles ***collide*** more frequently
pressure	reactions involving ***gases*** only	an increase in the pressure	greatly ***increases*** the rate of reaction – the effect is the same as that of an increase in ***concentration***
temperature	all reactions	an increase in temperature – this means that molecules are moving ***faster*** and collide more ***often (frequently)***; the particles also have more ***energy*** when they collide	***increases*** the rate of reaction
particle size	reactions involving solids and liquids, solids and gases or mixtures of solids	use the same mass of a solid but make pieces of solid ***more powdered (more broken up)***	greatly increases the rate of reaction
light	a number of photochemical reactions including photosynthesis, the reaction between methane and chlorine, and the reaction on photographic film	reaction in the presence of ***sunlight*** or UV light	greatly increases the rate of reaction
using a catalyst	slow reactions can be speeded up by adding a suitable catalyst	reduces amount of ***energy*** required for the reaction to take place: the catalyst is present in the same ***mass*** at the end of the reaction	***increases*** the rate of reaction

Exercise C6.3
The influence of surface area on the rate of reaction

a calcium carbonate + hydrochloric acid
→ calcium chloride + carbon dioxide + water

b Carbon dioxide is a gas and it escapes from the flask
through the cotton wool.

c

Time / s	0	30	60	90	120	150	180	210	240	270	300	330	360	390
Mass of CO_2 produced (expt. 1) / g	0.00	0.21	0.46	0.65	0.76	0.81	0.91	0.92	0.96	0.98	0.98	1.00	0.99	0.99
Mass of CO_2 produced (expt. 2) / g	0.00	0.51	0.78	0.87	0.91	0.94	0.96	0.98	0.99	0.99	0.99	1.00	0.99	1.00

d

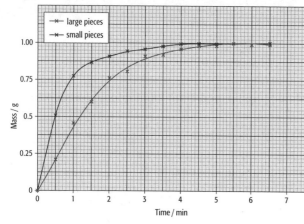

e The smaller pieces of marble (more powdered) gave the
faster rate of reaction because they have a greater surface
area in contact with the acid.

f The same volume of gas is produced in both cases
because all the conditions are the same in both cases –
the same mass of marble chips and the same volume and
concentration of acid are used each time.

Exercise C6.4
Finding the rate of a reaction producing a gas

a

Time / min	1	2	3	4	5	6
Volume of oxygen collected in experiment 1 / cm³	9	17	24	29	32	35
Volume of oxygen collected in experiment 2 / cm³	*21*	*35*	*43*	*48*	50	50

b

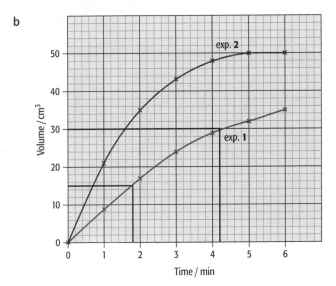

f Copper would appear to be the better catalyst as it produces the higher rate of reaction.

g The mass of copper at the end of the experiment should be the same as that at the start. A catalyst is not used up by the reaction it catalyses.

h The catalyst itself could be ground up (powdered) more finely; the temperature could be raised.

d Experiment 2 was the first to reach completion as no more gas was produced after 5 minutes.

Time taken to produce 30 cm³ / min	4.2
Time taken to produce 15 cm³ / min	1.8
Time taken to double the volume from 15 cm³ to 30 cm³ / min	2.4

Experiment 1 (using manganese(IV) oxide)

e Experiment 1: 20 cm³ are produced in 2.5 minutes
rate of reaction = 20/2.5 = 8 cm³ per minute
Experiment 2: 40 cm³ are produced in 2.5 minutes
rate of reaction = 40/2.5 = 16 cm³ per minute

Exercise C7.1
Acid and base reactions – neutralisation

All salts are ionic compounds. Salts are produced when an alkali neutralises an *acid*. In this reaction, the salt is formed when a *metal* ion or an ammonium ion from the alkali replaces one or more *hydrogen* ions of the acid. Salts can be crystallised from the solution produced by the neutralisation reaction. The salt crystals formed often contain *water* of crystallisation. These salts are called *hydrated* salts. The salt crystals can be heated to drive off the *water* of crystallisation. The salt remaining is said to be *anhydrous*.

Salts can be made by other reactions of acids. Magnesium sulfate can be made by reacting magnesium carbonate with *sulfuric* acid. The gas given off is *carbon dioxide*. Water is also formed in this reaction.

All *sodium* salts are soluble in water. Insoluble salts are usually prepared by *precipitation*.

Exercise C7.2 Types of salt

a **i** Hydrochloric acid always produces **chlorides**.

ii Nitric acid always produces **nitrates**.

iii Ethanoic acid always produces **ethanoates**.

iv Phosphoric acid always produces **phosphates**.

b

Substances reacted together		Salt produced	Other products of the reaction
dilute hydrochloric acid	zinc oxide	**zinc chloride**	**water**
dilute sulfuric acid	**copper carbonate**	copper sulfate	water and carbon dioxide
dilute sulfuric acid	**magnesium carbonate**	magnesium sulfate	water and carbon dioxide
dilute hydrochloric acid	**magnesium**	magnesium chloride	hydrogen
dilute nitric acid	copper oxide	**copper nitrate**	**water**
dilute ethanoic acid	**sodium hydroxide**	sodium ethanoate	water
dilute phosphoric acid	potassium hydroxide	potassium phosphate	**water**

Exercise C7.3
Descaling a coffee machine

a calcium carbonate + hydrochloric acid → calcium chloride + water + carbon dioxide

$$CaCO_3 + 2HCl \rightarrow CaCl_2 + H_2O + CO_2$$

b calcium citrate

c **i** HCl is too strong and may attack the metal of the machine.

   ii Ethanoic acid may leave a taste of vinegar in the coffee.

d **i** H_3NSO_3. It is used as a descaler and rust remover.

   ii 'Hard water' occurs in some areas, depending on the minerals present in the rocks through which the water passes in the area. It contains high levels of calcium or magnesium hydrogencarbonates. Mention of limestone areas. On heating, the calcium hydrogencarbonate decomposes to give insoluble calcium carbonate (limescale).

Exercise C7.4
Thermochemistry – investigating the neutralisation of an acid by an alkali

a

Volume of added NaOH(aq) / cm³	Temperature recorded / °C
0	21.0
10	28.0
20	35.0
30	35.0
40	31.0
50	30.0
60	27.5

b and c

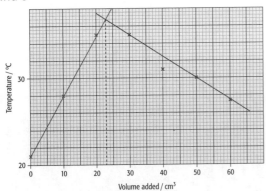

d the temperature after adding 40 cm³ of acid

e 23 cm³ (22.0–24.0 cm³ depending on lines drawn); it is the point where the two extrapolated lines meet

f The solutions are left to stand so that they are both at the same starting temperature (room temperature).

g Polystyrene is a good insulator and does not let heat from the reaction escape to the surroundings. It is a better insulator than glass.

h Improvements:

- the solutions could be more accurately measured out using a pipette or burette
- a more accurate thermometer could be used (one that reads to 0.1 °C)
- more values could be taken so that the graph could be more accurately drawn
- could use a lid on the polystyrene beaker to help retain heat
  (any **three** of these, and other sensible suggestions)

i sodium hydroxide + nitric acid → sodium nitrate + water

$$NaOH + HNO_3 \rightarrow NaNO_3 + H_2O$$

j exothermic

k $1.0 \times \dfrac{25.0}{1000} = 0.025$ moles

l from equation: 1 mole of sodium hydroxide reacts with 1 mole of nitric acid, therefore 0.025 moles NaOH will react with **0.025 moles of nitric acid**

m from experiment: there are 0.025 moles of acid in 23.0 cm³ of solution concentration of acid solution = $0.025 \times \dfrac{1000}{23.0}$ = 1.09 moles per dm³ = **1.1 moles per dm³** (to 2 significant figures)

117

Exercise C8.1
Trends in the halogens

a

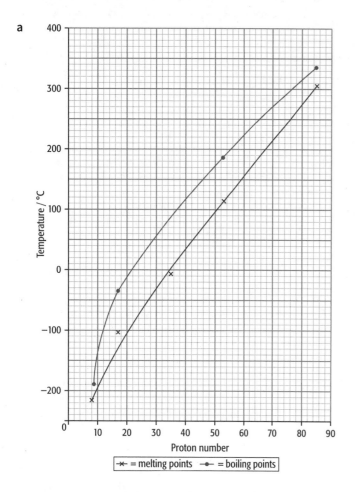

b estimated boiling point = 95–115 °C (actual value 114 °C)

colour: red-brown

physical state: liquid

c fluorine and chlorine

d solid, black

e The melting points increase as you go down the group.

Exercise C8.2
Displacement reactions of the halogens

a

Test Solution	Add chlorine water; followed by hexane	Add bromine water; followed by hexane	Add aqueous iodine; followed by hexane
KCl(aq)		no reaction	no reaction
KBr(aq)	solution changes from colourless to brown; brown colour moves into hexane layer		no reaction
KI(aq)	solution changes from colourless to brown; purple colour moves into hexane layer	solution changes from colourless to brown; purple colour moves into hexane layer	

b iodine → bromine → chlorine

increasing reactivity →

118

Exercise C8.3
Group I: The alkali metals

a   Caesium is a grey solid which conducts electricity.

b   There is **one electron** in the outer shell of a caesium atom.

c

Group I metal	Density/ g/cm^3	Radius of metal atom/nm	Boiling point / °C	Reactivity with water
sodium	0.97	0.191	883	floats and fizzes quickly on the surface, disappears gradually and does not burst into flame
potassium	0.86	0.235	760	*reacts instantly, fizzes and bursts into flame, may spit violently*
rubidium	1.53	0.250	686	reacts instantaneously, fizzes and bursts into flame then spits violently and may explode
caesium	1.88	*0.255–0.265 (actual value 0.260)*	*620–650 (actual value 671)*	*reacts instantly and explosively*

d   caesium + water → caesium hydroxide + hydrogen

Exercise C9.1
The reactivity series of metals

a magnesium + steam (water) → magnesium oxide + hydrogen

b copper or silver (or another metal low in the series)

c iron, or zinc, or magnesium (not calcium or sodium, etc., because these are too reactive to be safe)

d

		zinc iron(II) sulfate solution	zinc copper(II) sulfate solution	iron copper(II) sulfate solution	silver copper(II) sulfate solution	copper silver nitrate solution
At start	colour of metal	grey	*grey*	silver-coloured	silver-coloured	*brown*
	colour of solution	pale green	*blue*	blue	blue	colourless
At finish	colour of metal	coated with metallic crystals	*coated with brown solid*	coated with brown solid	silver-coloured	coated with silver-coloured crystals
	colour of solution	colourless	*colourless*	pale green	blue	*blue*

e zinc > iron > copper > silver

f copper and palladium

g barium and lanthanum

h barium or lanthanum

i iron and chromium are transition metals

Exercise C9.2
Energy from displacement reactions

a

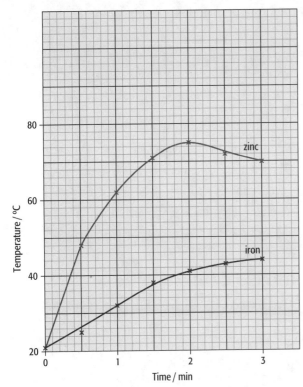

b iron + copper sulfate → iron sulfate + copper

Zn + CuSO$_4$ → ZnSO$_4$ + Cu

c zinc

d Zinc gave the higher temperature rise because it is the more reactive metal.

e This experiment would seem to be a 'fair test' although one difficulty would be whether the two metals were powdered to the same extent. Note that, although 5 g is not an equal number of moles of the two metals, it is an excess in both cases.

Exercise C9.3
Metals and alloys

a because it is quite a good conductor and is light; it has low density

b because aluminium is not very strong and the iron; steel core gives it more strength

c because copper is a better conductor and weight is not important

d because it is light and strong – it is also expensive so can only be used for specialist purposes

e It has a lower melting point and so it is easier to melt. It is also stronger and so the joints will be stronger.

f The pins of plugs have to be strong so Cu60 : Zn40 is used.

Brass instruments have to be shaped into tubes so a softer alloy is needed. Cu70 : Zn30 is therefore used.

Exercise C10.1
Atmospheric pollution, industry and transport

a power stations

b coal, natural gas, petroleum (crude oil)

c flue gas desulfurisers (scrubbers)

d **i** $N_2 + O_2 \rightarrow 2NO$

 ii $2NO + O_2 \rightarrow 2NO_2$

 iii The level of NO_x in the emissions from a diesel-engined car would be higher because the increased operating temperature would result in more reaction between nitrogen and oxygen from the air.

 iv a catalytic converter (catalyser)

e **i** The levels of these polluting gases would be higher in large cities because they are mainly produced by cars and other motor vehicles, and motor traffic is highest in large cities.

 ii lead – because modern cars now use lead-free petrol (gasoline)

f **i** drop for 2002 = 13.4% level at start of 2003 = 86.6% of original value drop for 2003 = 5,2% of 86.6 = 4.5% of original Total drop over two years = (13.4 + 4.5)% = 17.9%

 ii No, the benefits take place in the initial years following the introduction of the charge but then the reduction will level out.

 iii changes in vehicle and engine technology, including the type of fuel used, for example the introduction of hybrid and electric-powered cars

 The Congestion Charge Zone is not an isolated area / pollution can enter the area by being blown in by the wind / changes in human activity within the Congestion Charge Zone will affect the levels of vehicle usage in the area.

g The transport of containers by road requires a large number of vehicles – this means that they can be delivered to a large number of different destinations but with a resultant high level of emissions, including carbon dioxide.

 Transport by rail means that one locomotive can move a large number of containers – the level of emissions per container is less. There may need to be some road transport at the final destination but the distances involved, and therefore the level of emissions, would be less.

Exercise C10.2
Clean water is crucial

a Screens are used to filter away floating large items of rubbish, for example pieces of wood, logs, debris.

b Chlorine and; or ozone disinfect the water; they kill bacteria and microorganisms.

c Ozone breaks down/oxidises pesticides and other harmful chemicals.

d It is an oxidising agent.

e **i** the removal of salt(s) from solution

 ii distillation, reverse osmosis

 iii They are expensive, requiring large amounts of energy and sophisticated equipment.

f **i** test: acidify the tap water with a few drops of nitric acid and then add silver nitrate solution

 positive result: a white precipitate (of silver chloride) is seen

 ii sodium chloride + silver nitrate → silver chloride + sodium nitrate

 $NaCl + AgNO_3 \rightarrow AgCl + NaNO_3$

 iii $Ag^+(aq) + Cl^-(aq) \rightarrow AgCl(s)$

C11:
Carbonates

Exercise C11.1
The action of heat on carbonates

a   thermal decomposition

b   carbon dioxide; the test is to bubble the gas into limewater, and the limewater will turn milky if the gas is carbon dioxide (a white precipitate is produced)

c

Metal	Name of metal
A	copper
B	magnesium
C	calcium
D	sodium
E	zinc

d $ZnCO_3 \rightarrow ZnO + CO_2$

Exercise C11.2   Concrete chemistry

a   thermal decomposition

b $CaO + H_2O \rightarrow Ca(OH)_2$

c   The pH steadily increases from the surface of the beam (pH 7), through regions of pH 9, to pH 13 in the centre of the beam. This is because the alkaline calcium hydroxide at the surface is neutralised by the CO_2 in the air. Some carbon dioxide moves into the cracks to lower the pH a little there, but it cannot reach to the centre of the beam.

d   Limestone is used in the blast furnace in the manufacture of iron and in the manufacture of glass.

Exercise C12.1
Families of hydrocarbons

a The chief source of organic compounds is the naturally occurring mixture of hydrocarbons known as **petroleum**. Hydrocarbons are compounds that contain carbon and **hydrogen** only. There are many hydrocarbons because of the ability of carbon atoms to join together to form long **chains**. There is a series of hydrocarbons with just single covalent bonds between the carbon atoms in the molecule. These are saturated hydrocarbons, and they are called **alkanes**. The simplest of these saturated hydrocarbons has the formula CH_4 and is called **methane**. Unsaturated hydrocarbons can also occur. These molecules contain at least one carbon–carbon **double** bond. These compounds belong to the **alkenes**, a second series of hydrocarbons. The simplest of this 'family' of unsaturated hydrocarbons has the formula C_2H_4, and is known as **ethene**.

The test for an unsaturated hydrocarbon is to add the sample to **bromine** water. It changes colour from orange-brown to **colourless** if the hydrocarbon is unsaturated.

b

Name	Formula	Boiling point / °C
ethene	C_2H_4	−102
propene	C_3H_6	−48
butene	C_4H_8	−7
pentene	C_5H_{10}	30
hexene	C_6H_{12}	60 (58–62)

c relative molecular mass = 168; general formula C_nH_{2n}

formula **$C_{12}H_{24}$**

Exercise C12.2
Unsaturated hydrocarbons (the alkenes)

a

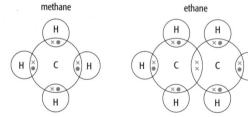

b $C_{10}H_{16}$

c The colour changes from orange-brown to colourless (not 'clear').

d **A** = thermometer

B = (water-cooled) condenser; Liebig condenser

C = measuring cylinder

e burning in an insufficient (limited) supply of air (or oxygen)

f Carbon monoxide is toxic because it interferes with the transport of oxygen in the body (by the blood).

g **i** C **ii** B

h

methane   ethane

× carbon electrons
• hydrogen electrons

Exercise C12.3
The alcohols as fuels

a $C_nH_{2n+1}OH$

b $C_2H_4 + H_2O \rightarrow C_2H_5OH$

conditions: 300 °C, 60 atm with phosphoric acid as catalyst

c

- air-lock containing water
- bubbles of carbon dioxide
- glucose solution and yeast

d Ethanol is toxic to the yeast and as more is produced it eventually kills the yeast.

e Ethanol is a product of anaerobic respiration – in the presence of oxygen a different reaction takes place / in the presence of oxygen the ethanol may be oxidised.

f carbon dioxide and water

g The raw material, ethene, is obtained from cracking petroleum fractions – a non-renewable resource.

Glucose can be obtained from sugar cane (or sugar beet) and so is a renewable resource.

h

i $C_2H_5OH + 3O_2 \rightarrow 2CO_2 + 3H_2O$

j $x = \dfrac{13.8}{2.3} \cdot 2.7 = 16.2\,g$ of water

k

l 0.58 g

m The same value was chosen so that an easy comparison could be made between the different alcohols – to make the experiments with the different alcohols easily/directly comparable.

Exercise C12.4
Essential processes of the petrochemical industry

a

Fraction	Name	Major use
A	refinery gas	as a fuel
B	gasoline (petrol)	fuel for cars
C	naphtha	for making chemicals
D	diesel oil / gas oil	used as fuel in diesel engines
E	bitumen	tar for road surfaces

b the different boiling points of the fractions

c 'Cracking' is the breakdown of long-chain hydrocarbons (alkanes) into shorter alkanes, usually with the production of an alkene as another product.

d The demand for particular fractions does not match the proportions of the different fractions in the starting petroleum – there is less demand for the longer-chain fractions so these are cracked to give the shorter molecules for which there is a greater demand.

e **i** $C_{15}H_{32} \rightarrow C_{12}H_{26} + C_3H_6$

ii

$$H-\overset{\overset{\displaystyle H}{|}}{\underset{\underset{\displaystyle H}{|}}{C}}-\overset{\overset{\displaystyle H}{|}}{\underset{\underset{\displaystyle H}{|}}{C}}=\overset{\overset{\displaystyle H}{|}}{C}$$

Exercise C12.5
Addition polymerisation

a Poly(ethene) is a **polymer** formed by the **addition** of **ethene** molecules. In this reaction, the starting molecules can be described as **monomers**; the process is known as **polymerisation**.

b

$$-\overset{\overset{\displaystyle H}{|}}{\underset{\underset{\displaystyle H}{|}}{C}}-\overset{\overset{\displaystyle H}{|}}{\underset{\underset{\displaystyle H}{|}}{C}}-\overset{\overset{\displaystyle H}{|}}{\underset{\underset{\displaystyle H}{|}}{C}}-\overset{\overset{\displaystyle H}{|}}{\underset{\underset{\displaystyle H}{|}}{C}}-\overset{\overset{\displaystyle H}{|}}{\underset{\underset{\displaystyle H}{|}}{C}}-\overset{\overset{\displaystyle H}{|}}{\underset{\underset{\displaystyle H}{|}}{C}}-$$ (this shows three repeat units)

C13:
Analysis

Exercise C13.1
Titration analysis

a There are situations when chemists need to know how much of a substance is present or how concentrated a solution of a substance is. This type of experiment is part of what is known as **quantitative** analysis. One experimental method used here is titration.

The important pieces of apparatus used in titration are a burette and a **pipette**. When an acid is titrated against an alkali, methyl orange can be used as the **indicator** so that we know that the acid has just **neutralised** the alkali. A few drops of **thymolphthalein** can be used as an alternative to methyl orange.

The experiment is repeated several times, often until **three** results have been obtained that are in close agreement to each other.

b **i**

Titration number	1	2	3	4
Final burette reading / cm³	25.9	48.6	32.4	28.5
First burette reading / cm³	0.0	23.3	6.9	3.1
Volume of solution A / cm³	25.9	25.3	25.5	25.4
Best titration results (✓)		✓	✓	✓

Tick (✓) the best titration results.

Using these results, the average volume of **A** was **25.4** cm³.

ii number of moles $= 0.0200 \times \dfrac{25.4}{1000} = 5.08 \times 10^{-4}$

iii a redox reaction (an oxidation–reduction reaction)

iv pale green to purple

Exercise C13.2
Chemical analysis

a **i**

Test	Observation	Conclusion
1 Solid **A** was dissolved in water and the solution divided into three parts for tests **2**, **3** and **4**.	*The white solid dissolved to give a colourless solution.*	**A** does not contain a transition metal.
2 **i** To the first part, aqueous sodium hydroxide was added until a change was seen.	*A white precipitate was formed.*	**A** may contain Zn^{2+} ions or Al^{3+} ions.
ii Excess aqueous sodium hydroxide was added to the mixture from **i**.	*The precipitate dissolved.*	
3 **i** To the second part, aqueous ammonia was added until a change was seen.	*A white precipitate was formed.*	The presence of Zn^{2+} ions is confirmed in **A**.
ii An excess of aqueous ammonia was added to the mixture from **i**.	*The precipitate dissolved in excess alkali.*	
4 *To the third part, a few drops of dilute nitric acid were added, followed by silver nitrate solution.*	*A yellow precipitate was formed.*	**A** contains I⁻ ions.

ii zinc iodide, ZnI_2

b **i**

Test	Observations
1 A sample of the solid mixture was dissolved in distilled water. The solution was acidified with dilute HCl(aq) and a solution of Ba(NO$_3$)$_2$ added.	A white precipitate was formed.
2 A sample of the solid was placed in a test tube. NaOH(aq) was added and the mixture warmed. A piece of moist red litmus paper was held at the mouth of the tube.	The solid dissolved and pungent fumes were given off. The litmus paper turned **blue**, indicating the presence of **ammonium** ions.
3 A sample of the solid was dissolved in distilled water to give a **colourless** solution. NaOH(aq) was added dropwise until in excess.	A **white** precipitate was formed which was **soluble** in excess alkali.
4 A further sample of the solid was dissolved in distilled water. Concentrated ammonia solution (NH$_3$(aq)) was added dropwise until in excess.	A **white** precipitate was formed. On addition of excess alkali, the precipitate was **soluble**.

ii ammonium sulfate ((NH$_4$)$_2$SO$_4$) and zinc sulfate, (ZnSO$_4$)

iii The precipitate in both tests is zinc hydroxide, (Zn(OH)$_2$).

c **i** observations for tests on filtrate:

  1 The filtrate is a colourless solution.

  2 A white precipitate is formed – the precipitate re-dissolves on adding excess sodium hydroxide to give a colourless solution.

  3 A white precipitate is formed – this precipitate does not re-dissolve in excess ammonia – the solution is colourless.

  4 No precipitate is formed on acidification and addition of silver nitrate.

  5 A white precipitate is formed when barium nitrate is added.

ii The gas is carbon dioxide.

iii Solid **Q** is a carbonate because carbon dioxide was produced with acid.

Solid **Q** is a calcium or magnesium compound because there is a white precipitate formed with NaOH(aq) which does not dissolve in excess alkali.

Solid **Q** is aluminium carbonate.

Exercise C13.3
Planning a controlled experiment

a plan should cover the following ideas: use same type of 'cloth' and stain; use same amount of washing powder; change temperature; stir; agitate for same length of time; compare cleanliness of samples, repeat to check

b plan should cover the following ideas: add each sample to (hot) water and stir; crush; filter solution, concentrate solution, place spots of each on paper; repeat to get deeper colour, again place spots on paper; chromatography, place in solvent (water or other), wait for separation, compare to see if the samples are the same or there are extra added spots in cheaper sample

c **i** plan should cover the following ideas: use each solvent separately, the same; measured amount of each; **then**:

  either add small measured quantities to each solvent separately; stirring until no more will dissolve then compare total masses

  or add excess (measured until no more will dissolve) to each solvent separately; stir, filter and weigh residue; subtract from total mass added; compare the two

ii Dissolve a sample of the old urea in the solvent with heating and stirring; filter the hot solution to remove any undissolved residue; collect the solution in an evaporating basin and heat to concentrate the solution; allow the solution to cool slowly; filter off the crystals that form and dry them between filter papers.

d i Dip some pieces of litmus paper (or Universal Indicator paper) into the two products and see which paper loses its colour; is bleached.

ii Take the non-bleach product; measure out a known volume; fractionally distil and measure the quantity of ethanol distilling over.

Exercise C13.4
Chemical testing and evaluation

a plan should cover the following ideas: crush samples and take equal masses of each; add acid until no further reaction takes place; filter the resulting solution; dry the residue and weigh it in each case; compare masses of impurities

b i K^+; Mg^{2+}; NO_3^-; HCO_3^-

ii flame test: yellow colour produced

iii pH paper or pH meter

iv Measure a known quantity of the water into a pre-weighed container; evaporate (boil) to dryness avoiding any of the liquid spitting out; cool and re-weigh; subtract the mass of container and compare with the stated mass.

c i Add sodium hydroxide until in excess; the white precipitate re-dissolves to form a colourless solution.

ii Add each metal separately to an equal volume of acid; **then**:

either time the reaction; measure the gas quantity given off and compare the time until completion; volume of gas given off in fixed time

or measure the temperature of the acid before addition; measure again at end; compare the temperature rise in each case.

d Take equal lengths; masses of magnesium ribbon; equal quantities; volumes of acid; use the same temperature for each test; need a method of changing concentration of the acid using suitable dilution (keeping the total volume the same); time the reaction to completion and compare times or measure the gas produced in a fixed time and compare the volumes produced; make a quantitative comparison or graph of the results.

Exercise C13.5
Experimental design

a The aim of this experiment is to investigate the effect of an increase in temperature on the rate of a chemical reaction. In this experiment, the faster the rate of reaction, the quicker the 'cross' will disappear.

For the results of the experiment at different temperatures to be compared fairly, the only condition that should change is the temperature. The following factors need to be kept constant:

- the concentrations of the solutions used

- the volumes of solutions used

- the dimensions of the conical flasks in which the reactions are carried out – the depth of solution that the experimenter looks through must be the same all the time.

The solutions must be stable at the temperature being studied – so they should stand in the thermostatically controlled water bath for a suitable period to adjust to temperature.

Safety goggles should be worn because acid is being used. Ideally the experiment should be carried out in a fume cupboard or well-ventilated room as sulfur dioxide gas is produced, which is an irritant.

The instructions should include an outline of the procedure:

- the mixing of appropriate volumes of solutions – measured using a clean measuring cylinder – at the right temperature

- when to consistently start timing – this should be after adding the second solution

- to mix the solutions thoroughly by swirling the flask

- to take the time at the immediate disappearance of the marked 'cross' and record it accurately.

b i

Experiment	Thermometer diagram	Initial temperature / °C	Thermometer diagram	Final temperature / °C	Average temperature / °C	Time for printed text to disappear / s
1		24		24	24	130
2		33		31	32	79
3		40		38	39	55
4		51		47	49	33
5		60		54	57	26

ii

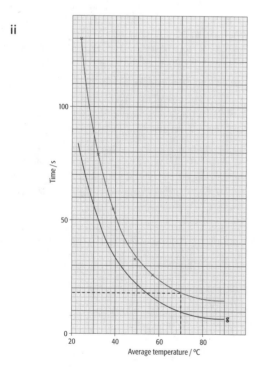

c Experiment **5**

d This was the experiment carried out at the highest temperature. Increasing the temperature increases the rate of a reaction because the particles are moving faster and therefore collide more frequently. They also have more energy when they collide and so are more likely to react.

e These conditions are necessary to make sure that the experiments can be fairly compared. If any of these were different between experiments then the observer would not be looking through the same depth of liquid to see when the cross disappeared.

f 16–20 seconds (a sensible range of time is allowed, as different people will draw a slightly different line between the points).

g The line will run beneath the curve for the original experiment as the reaction will be faster using a higher concentration of sodium thiosulfate (see blue curve on graph).

h Temperatures between 0 and 5 °C can be achieved using an iced-water bath or using solutions that have been cooled sufficiently in a refrigerator.

i More accurate control of the temperature can be achieved by carrying out the experiments in a thermostatically controlled water bath.